Heaven's Angels

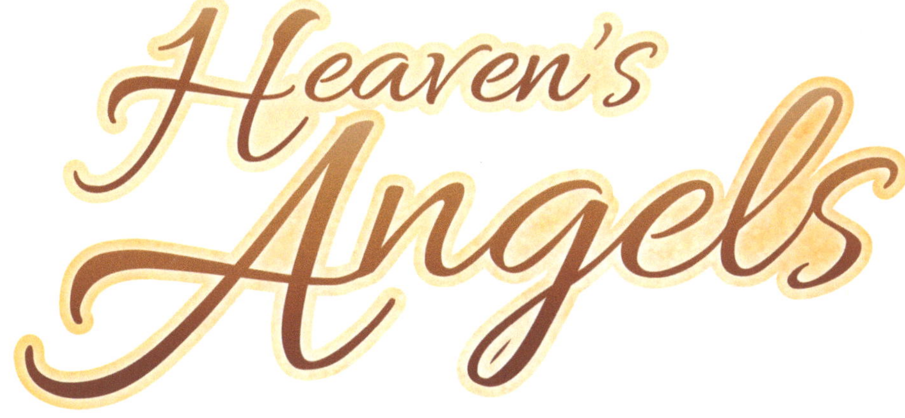

BASED ON
The Summa Theologica

WRITTEN BY
Carrie Magalski

ARTWORK BY
Dona Gelsinger

used with permission from Gelsinger Licensing Group

Dona Gelsinger

Edited by Jessica Bardin and Paula Martin

**Images are not meant to depict actual renditions of the angels, but rather to visually assist the imagination of the reader, since angels can assume a form deemed appropriate by God to the eye of the beholder.*

Dedication

This book is dedicated to my husband Jason and to our children Alina, Carina, Kristina, and Andrew; you are the love and light in our lives. To all God's children, know that you are loved, chosen, protected. You each have a special mission to fulfill in your life. Have peace knowing that He has great plans for you.

Published by
Biblio Publishing
BiblioPublishing.com

ISBN: 978-1-62249-294-7
Library of Congress Control Number: 2015916955

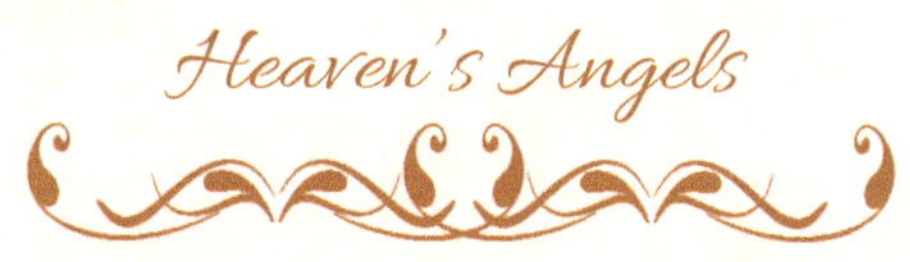

Table of Contents

Prologue

Dona Gelsinger is a world-renowned professional artist, who over three decades ago took our imaginations to the highest limit and lifted our spirits to be present in the Heavenly realm with her collection, "Heaven's Little Angels". In return, her gifted art has united angelic inspirations to our yearnings for hope and joy deep within the recesses of our hearts.

After years of research and inspiration from Dona Gelsinger's artwork, I present to you an exciting endeavor about the nine choirs of angels based on the teachings of St. Thomas Aquinas, known as the *Doctor of the Angels* in his best-known work, *The Summa Theologica*. This book will express these foundational truths of the angelic choirs in a visually and compelling way for all readers to understand. With the permission of Gelsinger Licensing Group for artist Dona Gelsinger, we have collaborated to use her artwork of "Heaven's Little Angels" to visually represent this teaching on the angels.

Since humanity needs to embrace the fundamental truth that God has created angels to guide us on earth, to keep order in the universe, and to continually Glorify Him in Heaven, our knowledge of this can be a moral compass for the essential growth of future generations. Based on Biblical accuracy and the Catechetical truth of the universality of angels and how they interacted with humans, this book capitalizes on the light and hope society longs for during this modern era. Imagine a training camp whereas according to the Divine Governance of the Summa (106) the *superior* angels enlighten or illuminate the *inferior* angels. The story of this creation is told through the eyes of Archangel Uriel,

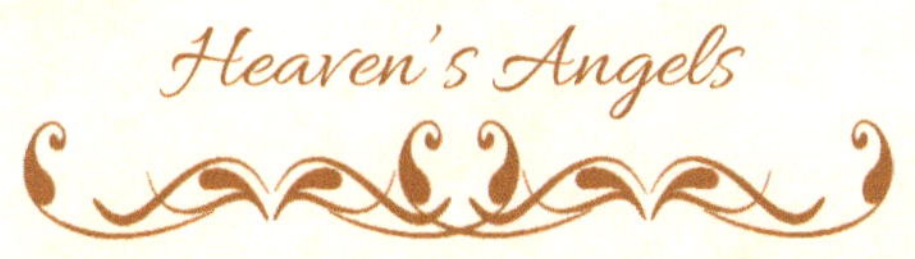

who is referenced in the apocryphal texts of the Bible and revered in early and modern Eastern Catholicism. Archangel Uriel takes the reader on this journey through creation and explains the missions of the angelic choirs as they pertain to the universe and mankind. He also inspires us with an insight that can only be perceived without the boundaries of space or time.

"Heaven's Angels" will awaken awareness that angels were created as God's messengers and our guardians, and we are never alone. Putting these words to Dona's artwork will *"bring the angels to life"* in the mind of the reader. The images are not meant to accurately depict the angels, but rather to assist the imagination, since God will allow the angels to take a form that is befitting according to the eye of the beholder.

Carrie Magalski's professional experience encompasses: author of inspirational articles, treatments for animations and commercials, and the eulogy for St. John Paul II in the movie, "The Seed of Faith"; featured blogger on Columbus Catholic Women's Blog; and writing legislation on burial laws in Ohio that honors life. Carrie is currently the Coordinator for Internships and Employer Relations at Ohio Dominican University and most recently worked in broadcast communications as the Public Relations, News Correspondent and Community Outreach Coordinator of St. Gabriel Radio, one of the largest Catholic radio stations in the country. She also serves as a board member for Back in His Arms Again, a ministry that helps families of infant loss.

For more information on the Angels visit:

heavensangelsbook.com

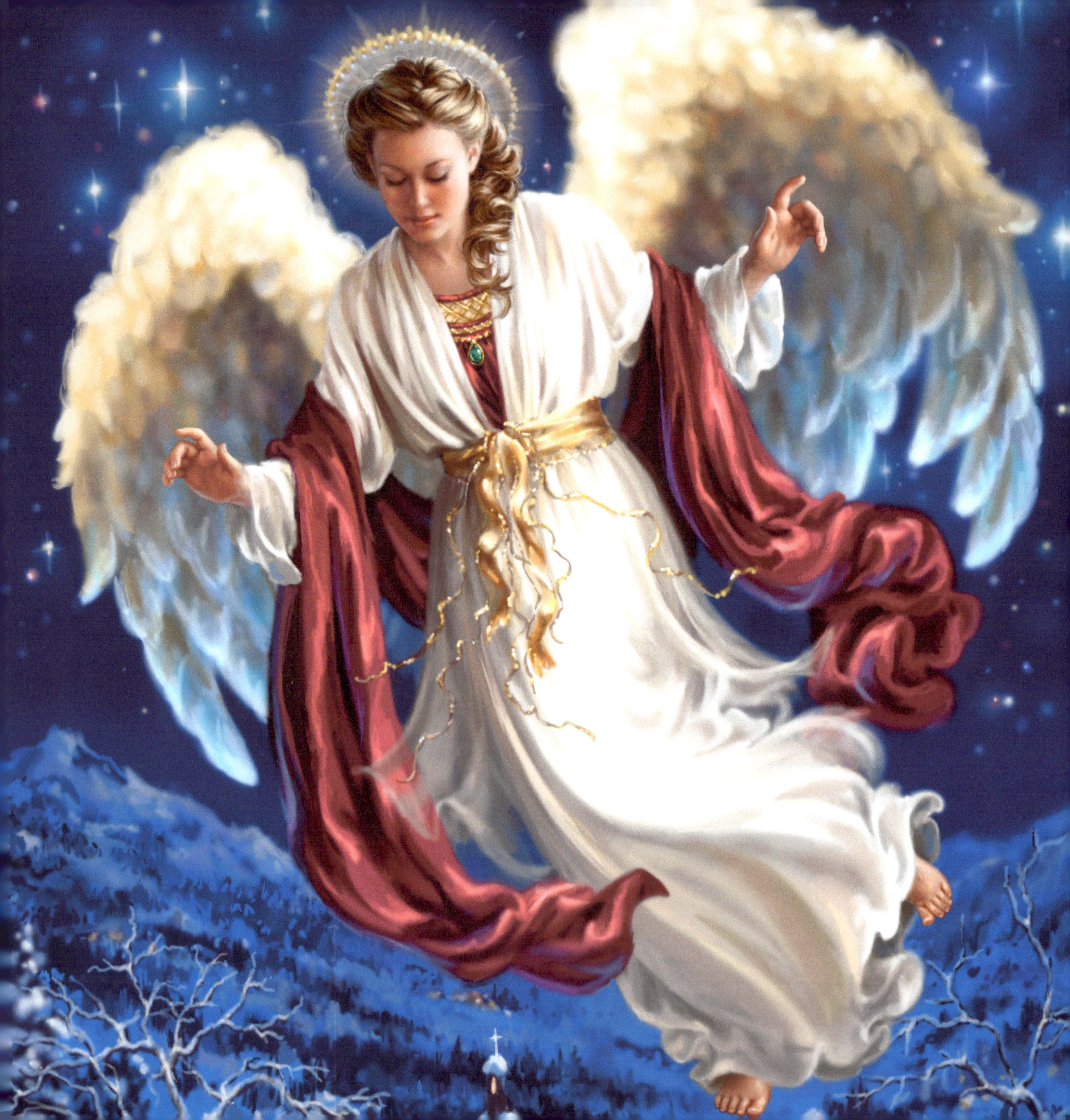

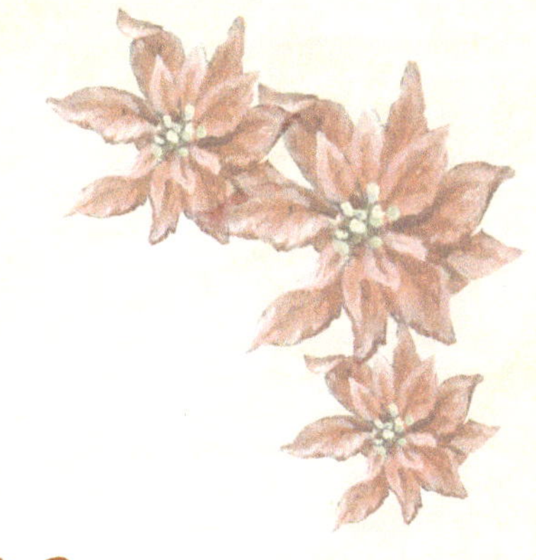

The Beginning

Before the creation of mankind, God created the universe. This universe was created out of chaos; to bring order to this chaos, God created nine angelic choirs of Angels. These Angels are behind the veil that exists between the spirit world and the physical world.

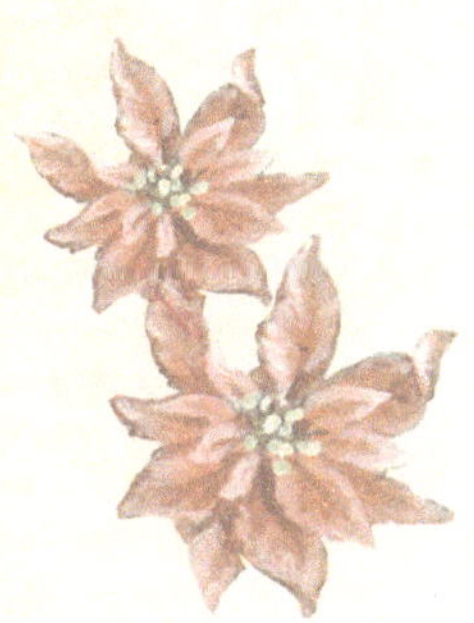

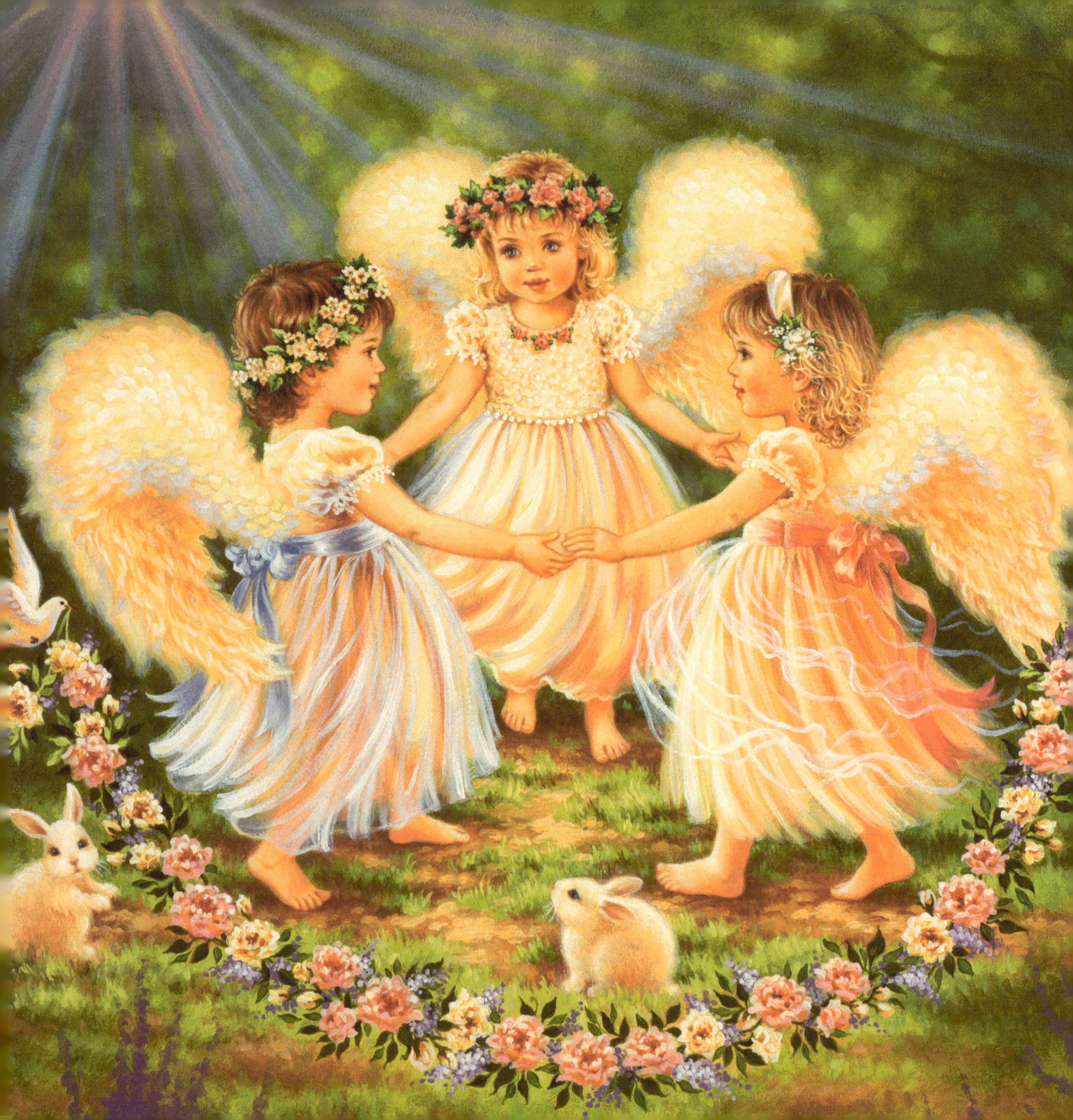

ngels can appear in any form that God allows, providing a clearer interpretation and understanding of His message. This is why angels can take the form of a beautiful motherly figure or the sweet innocence of a child. In the blink of an eye, the angel's free-will manifests its spirit into a glorious form that the eye can behold. Angels do not have physical bodies, but throughout biblical history they have assumed bodies in order to communicate with human beings.

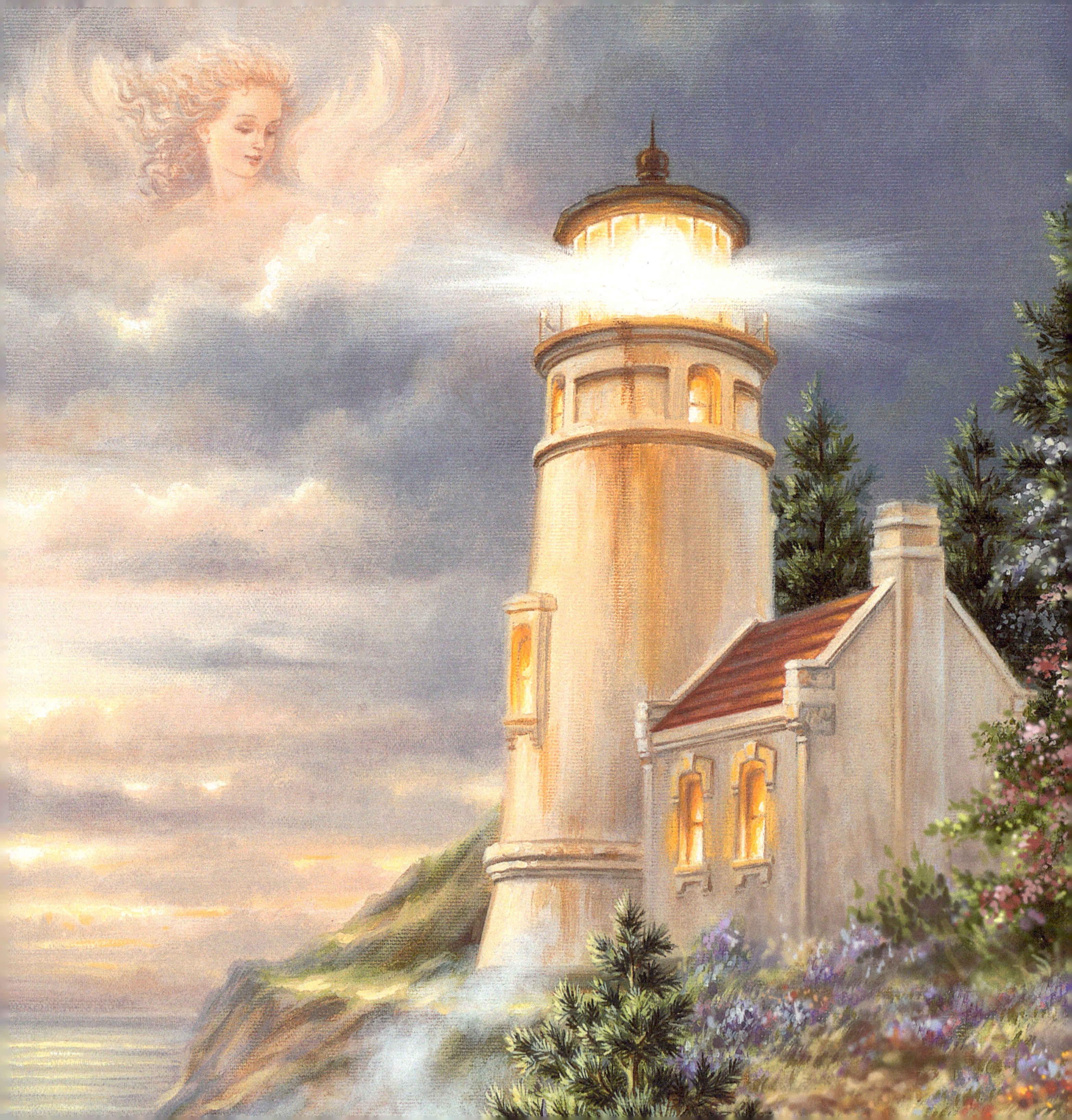

INTRODUCTION

My name is Archangel Uriel, which means "Fire of God." As the fourth Archangel who defends the Throne of God, it is my job to bring truth to the eyes of the beholder. I have roamed the heavens and the earth since the dawn of my creation and have seen the light and darkness in all things. I have endless, beautiful stories that weave together a tapestry of mankind, even in the wake of darkness and pain. In pain, there is hope and in hope, faith. God is always waiting as a light of hope in the depths of your despair. You just need to see His light.

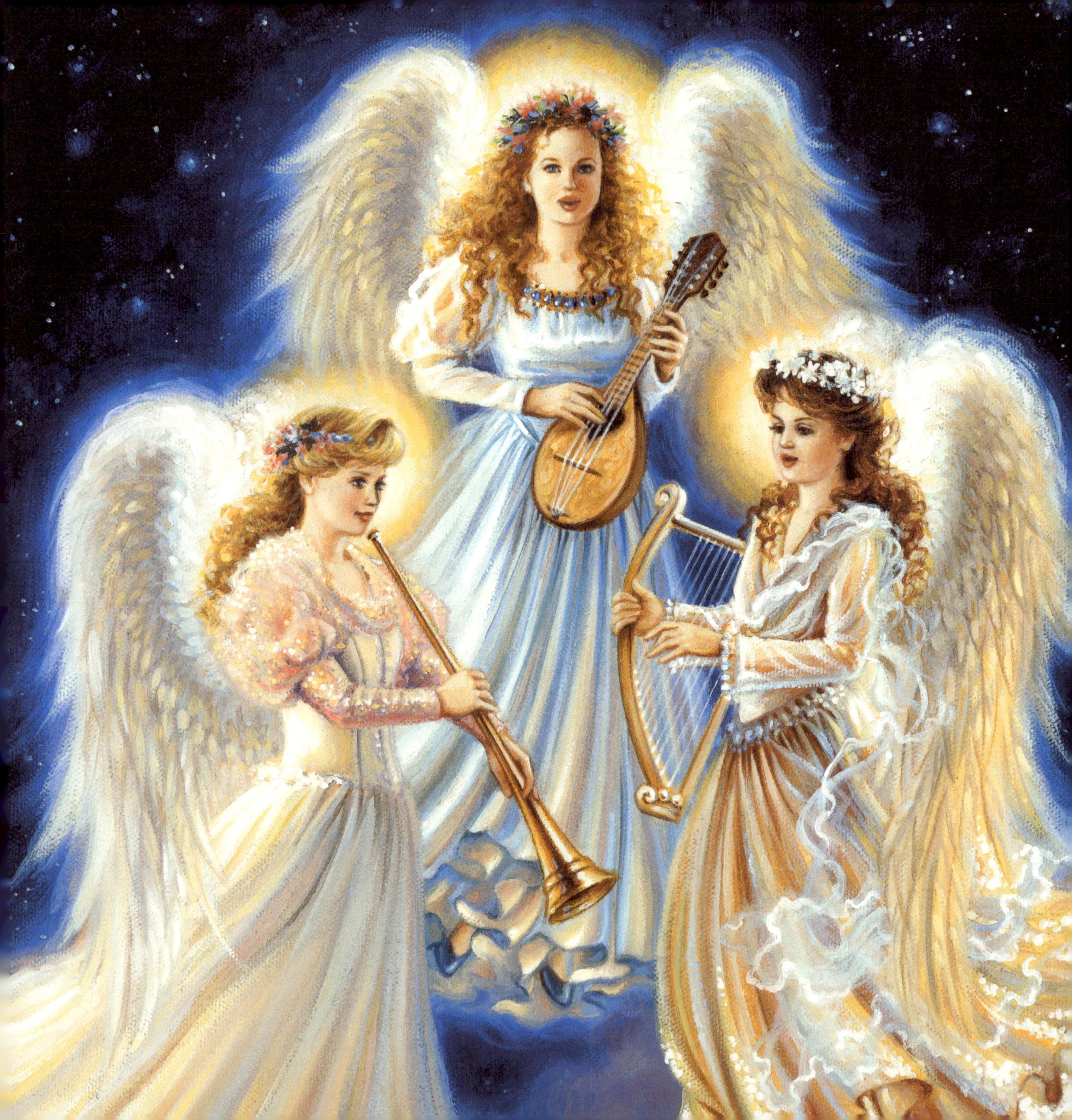

These timeless stories tell of the creation of the Heavenly Choirs of Angels whose ultimate goal is to assist souls in finding their way back to Heaven to be in communion with God. I, Archangel Uriel, will assist you in this journey. In the heavenly realm, God sits on His throne so high that it will be out of our sight when we are in His presence. The nine choirs of Angels have three hierarchies* based on how close they are to Our Creator.

levels based on rank

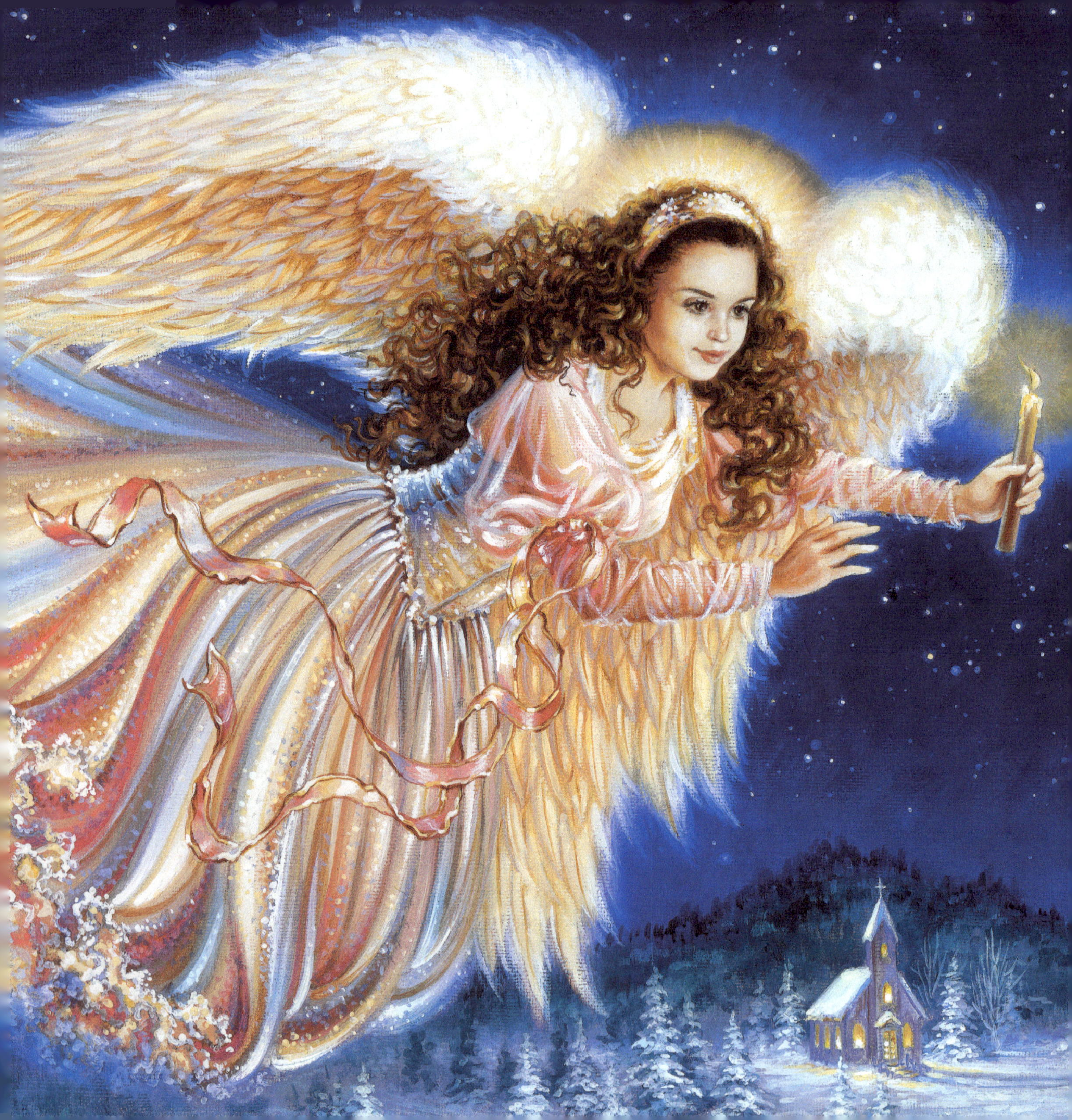

The first hierarchy has the privilege of being the closest to the Throne and has the most wisdom and knowledge with the sole purpose of glorifying God and eternally singing His praise. The second hierarchy has the privilege of keeping order in the universe and balance in creation. The third hierarchy assists mankind in all of its endeavors. These Angels keep watch over all the nations, communities, families, and every human being.

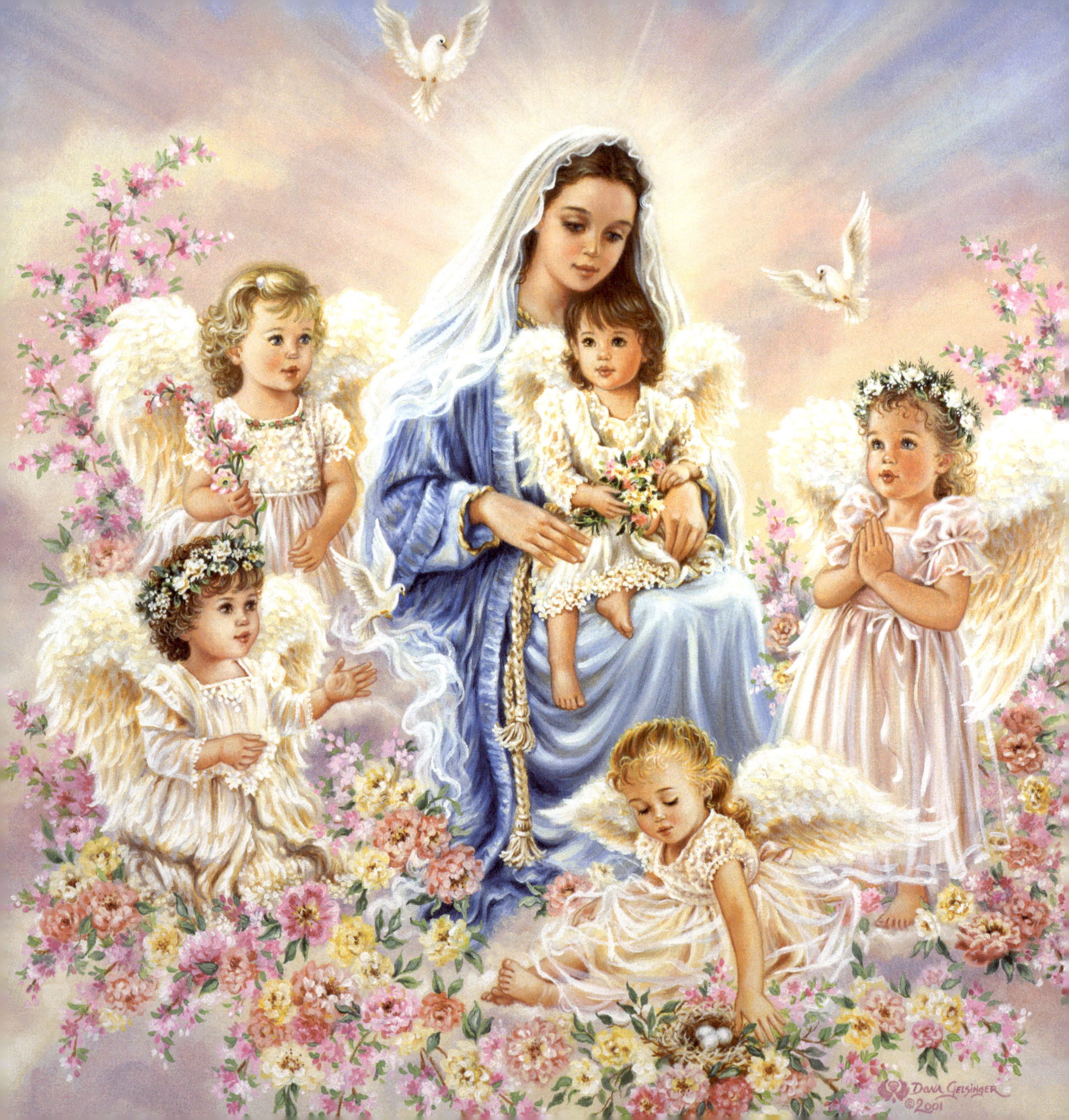

Dana Gelsinger
©2001

THE FIRST HIERARCHY

The Seraphim

As we soar to the great Throne of God, we see the highest choir of Angels, the **Seraphim**. These are the purest in spirit; their intense, burning love protects the whole cosmos. Their burning flame is the light that destroys the darkness. They continually contemplate God in all of His glory and they sing His constant praise. Their adoration radiates down to the other eight choirs of angels. The only creature close to them is the Queen of the Angels: the Mother of Jesus Christ who, with all her honor, imparts God's grace to all through the Seraphim. She sends the Seraphim down to gather the prayers of mankind and brings them to Her Son.

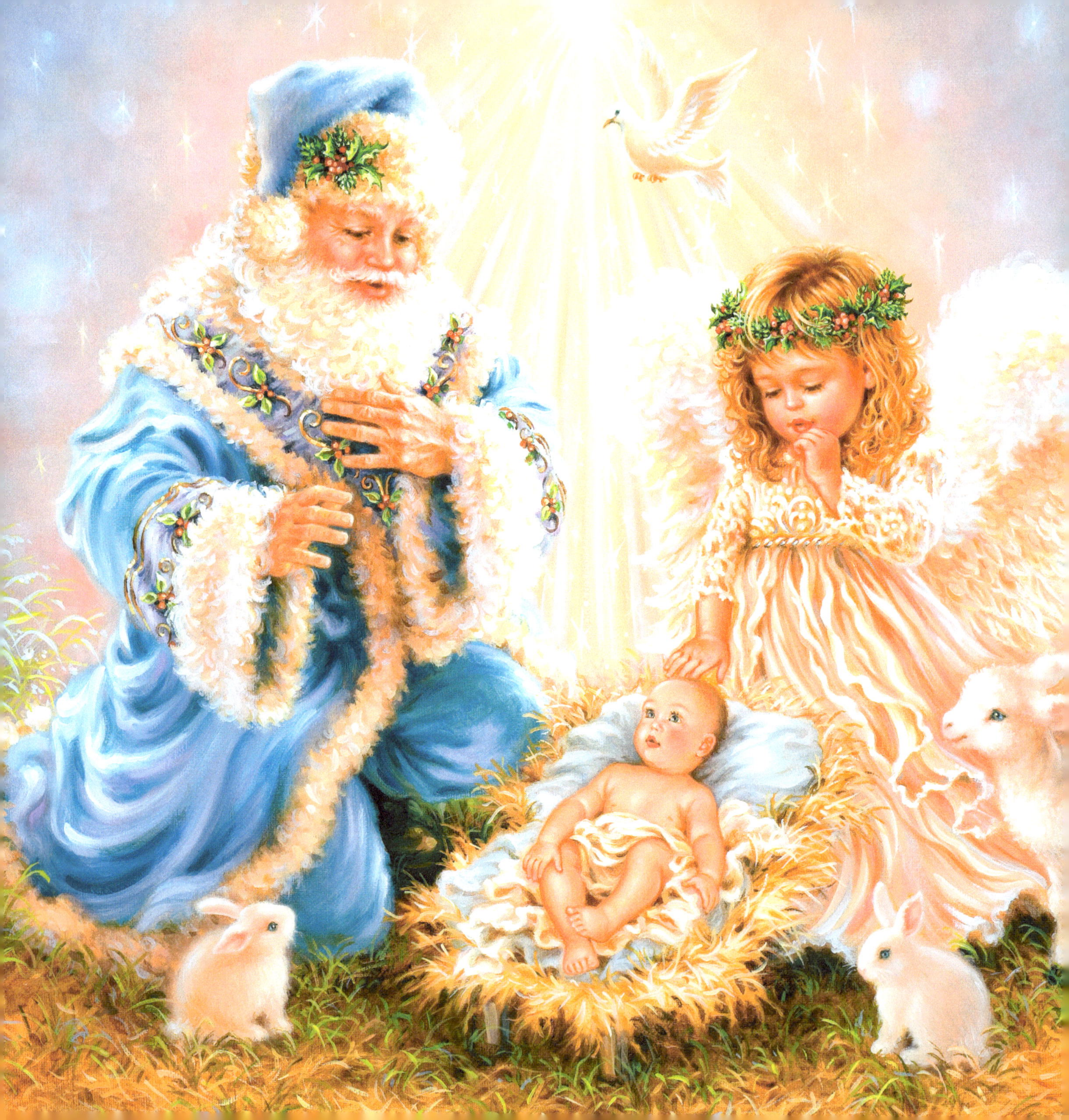

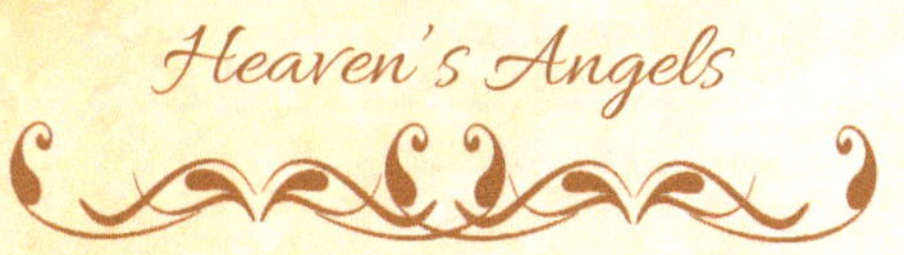

efore the beginning of time, Lucifer — known as the "Bearer of Light" — was created as a Seraphim. His pride became his downfall. God revealed His plan for His Son's incarnation so that man may have eternal salvation. Because he wanted to be like God, Lucifer refused to bow down to flesh and blood: *God made man.*

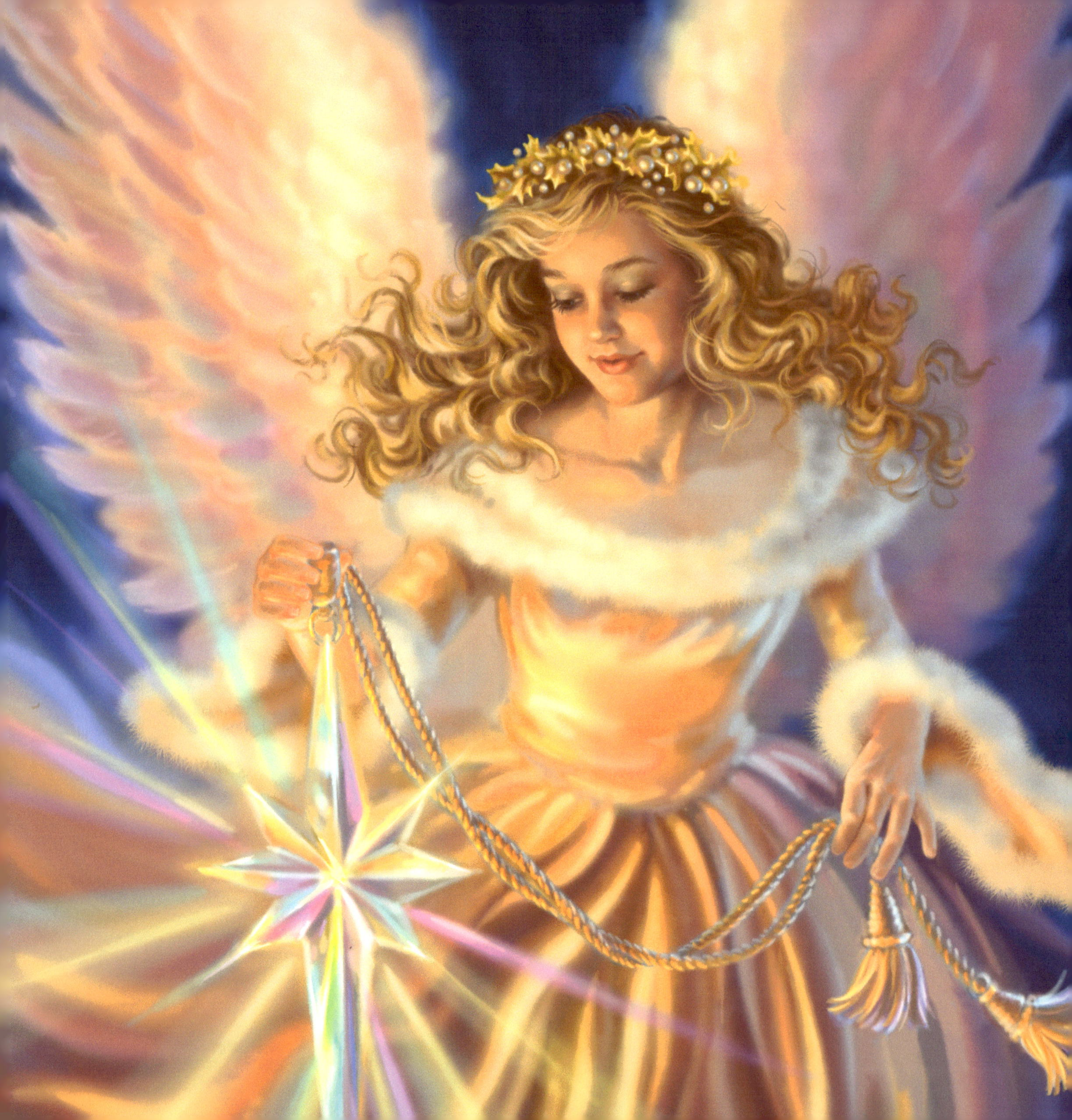

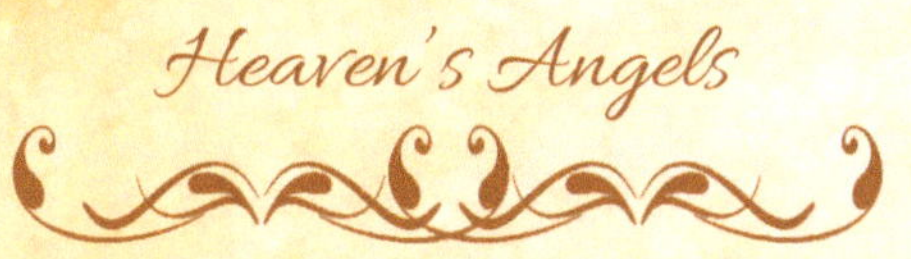

Then in an instant, there arose from the lower choir of Angels the mighty Archangel Michael. He cried out "Who is Like God," and with his whole mind and free-will chose to defend our Lord. At that moment, the great battle in Heaven occurred and a third of the Angels fell to earth with their leader Lucifer, never to return to Heaven. In this moment, all of angelic creation made the choice to love God or refuse Him, an eternal decision. Now here I, Uriel, stand with the other six Archangels protecting the Throne of our Lord and revealing the light of His Love to all of His creation.

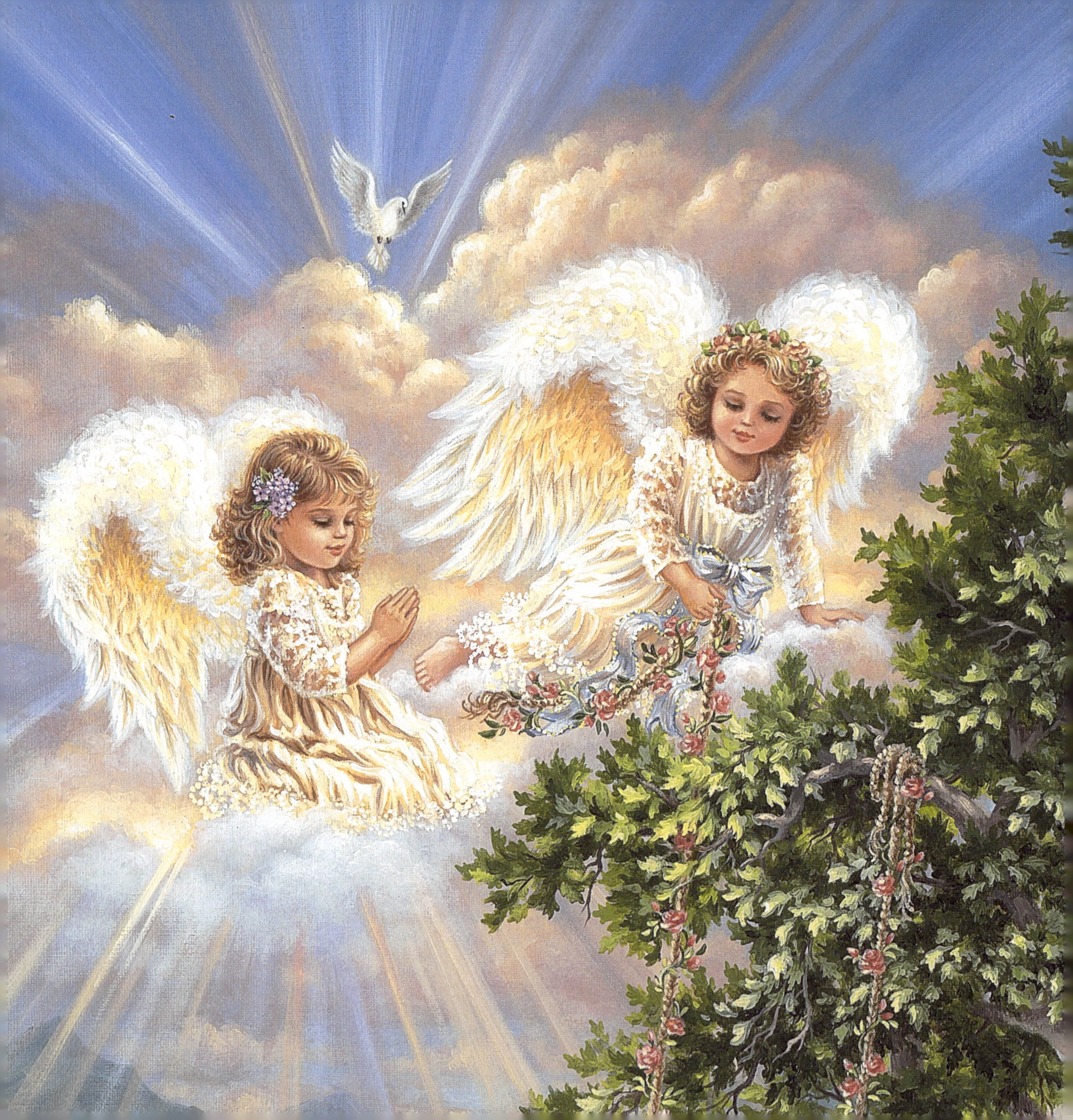

The Cherubim

The magnificence of God is greater than your imagination. The power of His love is what created the universe and all souls. The **Cherubim** are responsible for keeping record of God's creative powers. Their mission is to magnify the power and the holiness of The Almighty and contemplate His plan for creation. Their power is in knowing and beholding His eternal Wisdom and Light.

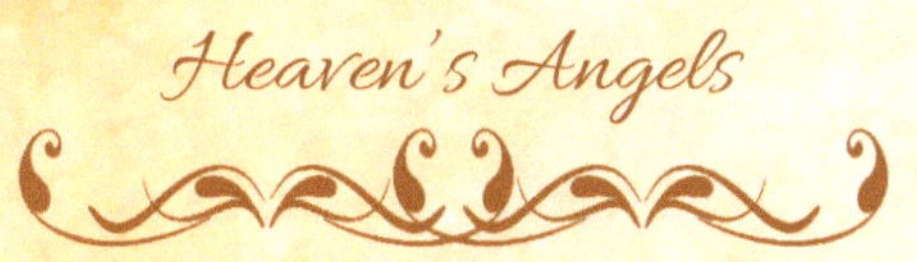

In the beginning of creation, Cherubim were placed with me at the gate of the Garden of Eden when God drove Adam and Eve out. He had given them Paradise and asked them not to eat of the Tree of Knowledge of good and evil. But through the temptation of Satan, who was cast out of Heaven, they disobeyed. Sin was set in Adam and Eve's hearts and Paradise was lost. With the fullness of knowledge and wisdom, the Cherubim act as heavenly counselors as they stand guard to the Tree of Knowledge and help mankind seek eternal truth.

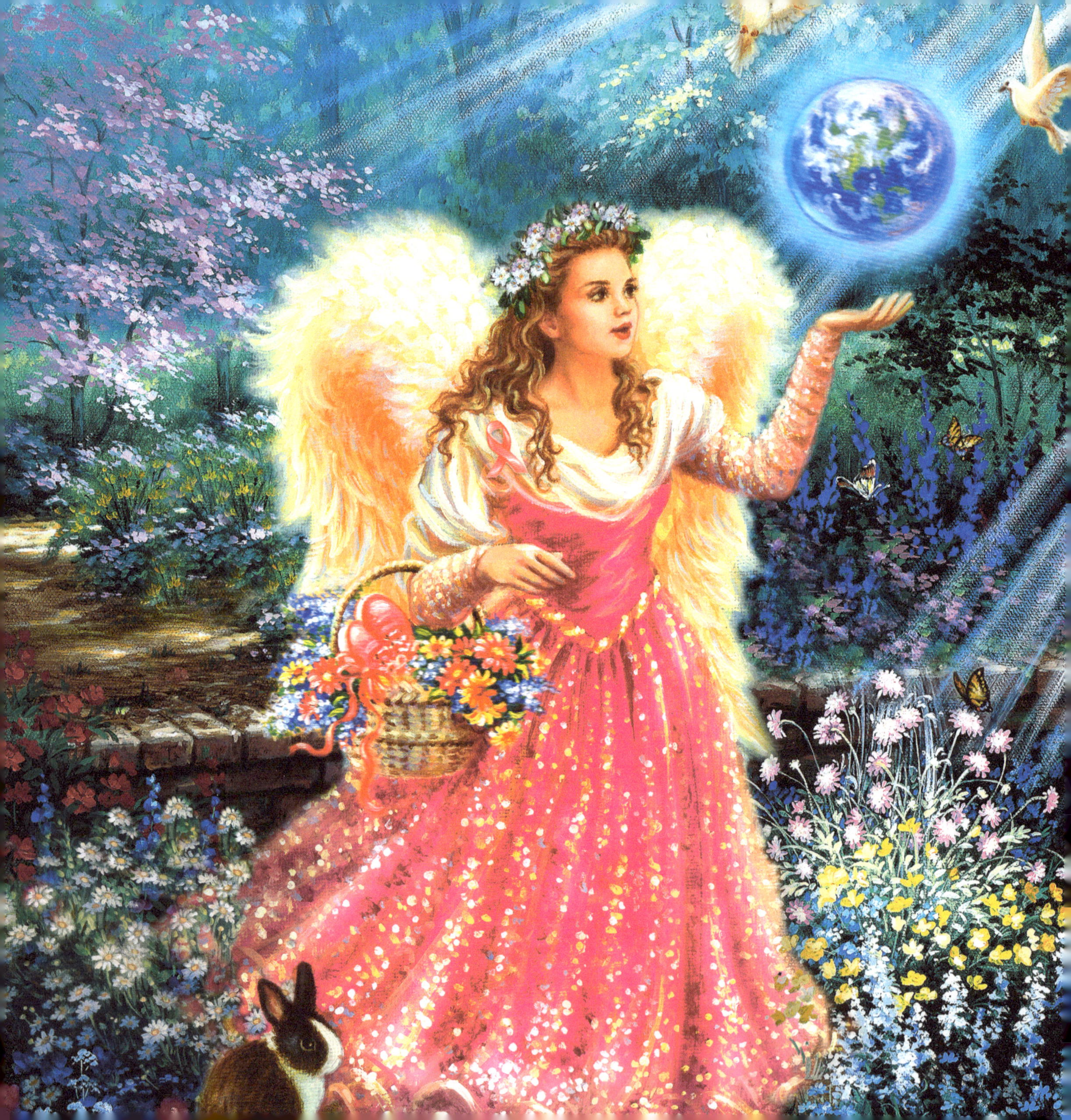

The Thrones

It is because of God's great love that His mercy is abundant. But even when He is merciful, there still needs to be judgment. The choir of **Thrones** mirrors God's great majesty and is responsible for carrying out God's great judgment according to spiritual and universal laws. Because of their humility they can hold the scales of justice, and their peace radiates down to the other choirs of Angels. They are considered friends of the planets because the material universe takes form where they exist. Therefore, no Angel from the lower hierarchies may attain the glorious presence of God without first passing through this choir of Angels.

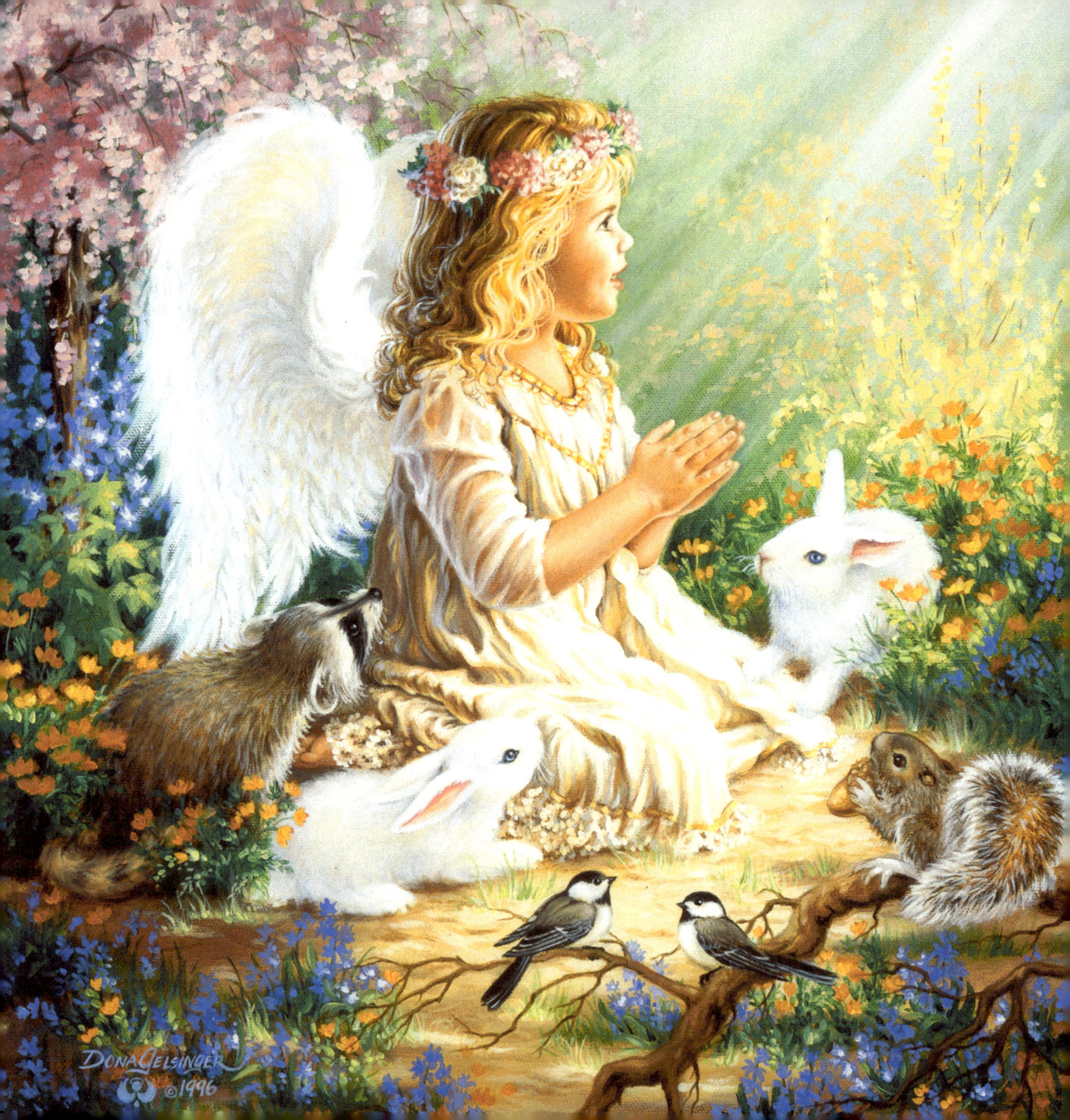

Dona Gelsinger
©1996

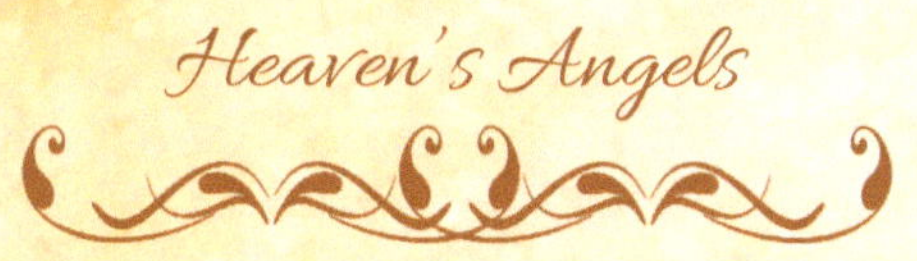

 aking flight into the darkness, I look out past my wingspan to see God's great creation before me. Even though the heavens and earth are in my sight, time and space separate the two; but what you don't know is that the beauty is still there beyond the veil. You just need to believe. I rush past the streets of translucent gold and sparkling gemstones to a place where the heavens transcend the imagination. Mortal eyes have never beheld the immense colors that you will one day see illuminated by the brightest light that will immerse your soul. You were made in His image and likeness to feel this joy and love and to be in perfect union with Him.

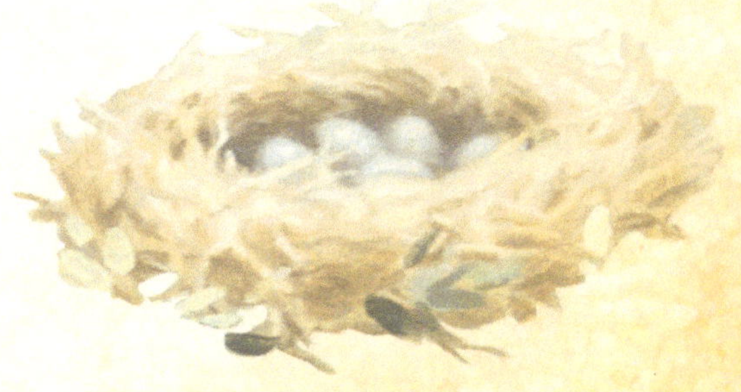

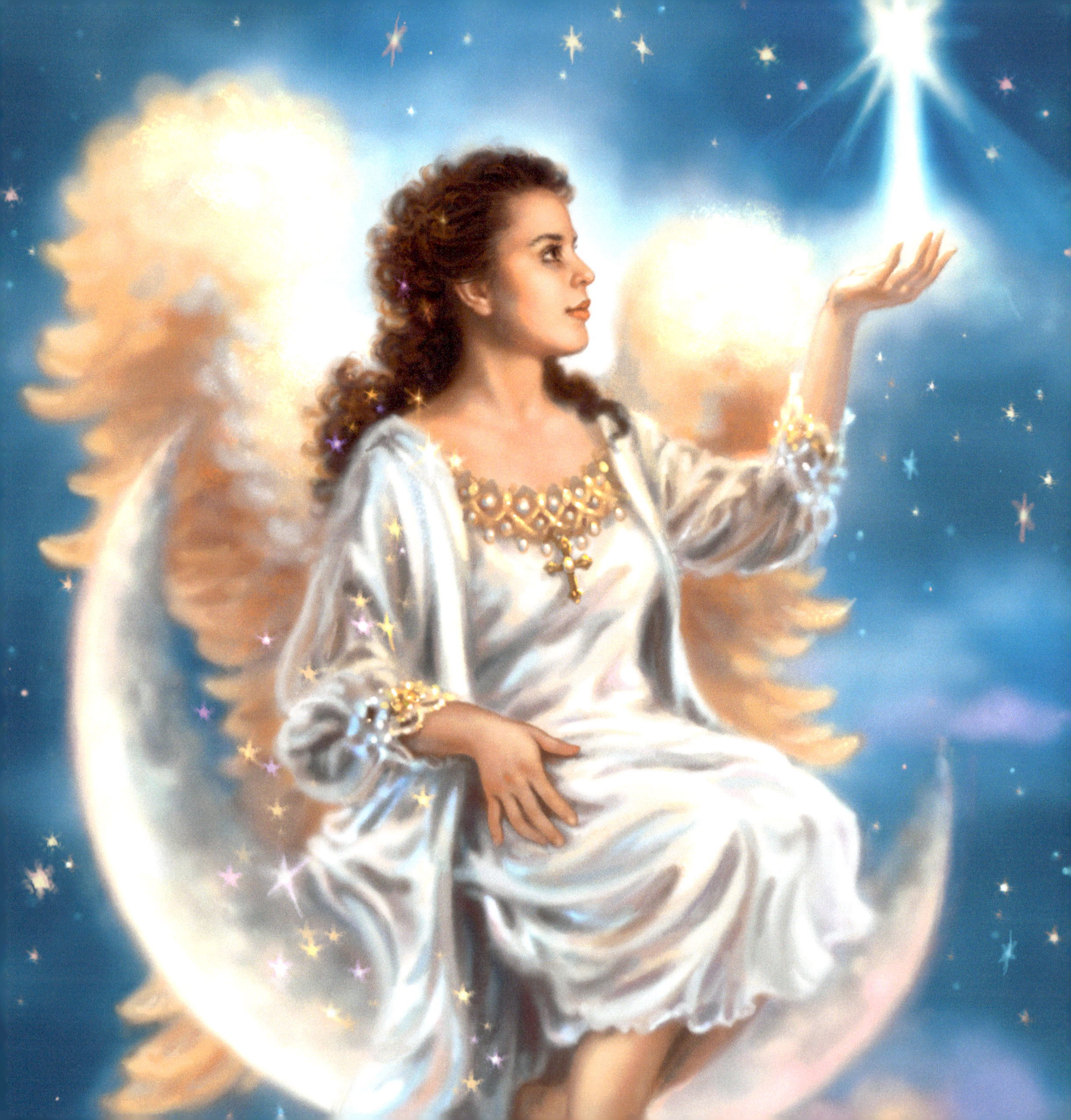

THE SECOND HIERARCHY
The Dominions

As your eyes gaze up into the vast galaxy above you, do you ever wonder how the planets move about or what is keeping the stars in place? The **Dominions** ensure that the other choirs of Angels are carrying out God's Will. Each and every star has an Angel that beholds it there and every planet has an Angel that moves it through the solar system. This choir of Angels keeps balance between the material and spiritual worlds. They keep the balance of power by appointing those things that are to be accomplished by the other Virtues and Powers. They ensure that the wisdom of God is being carried out accordingly.

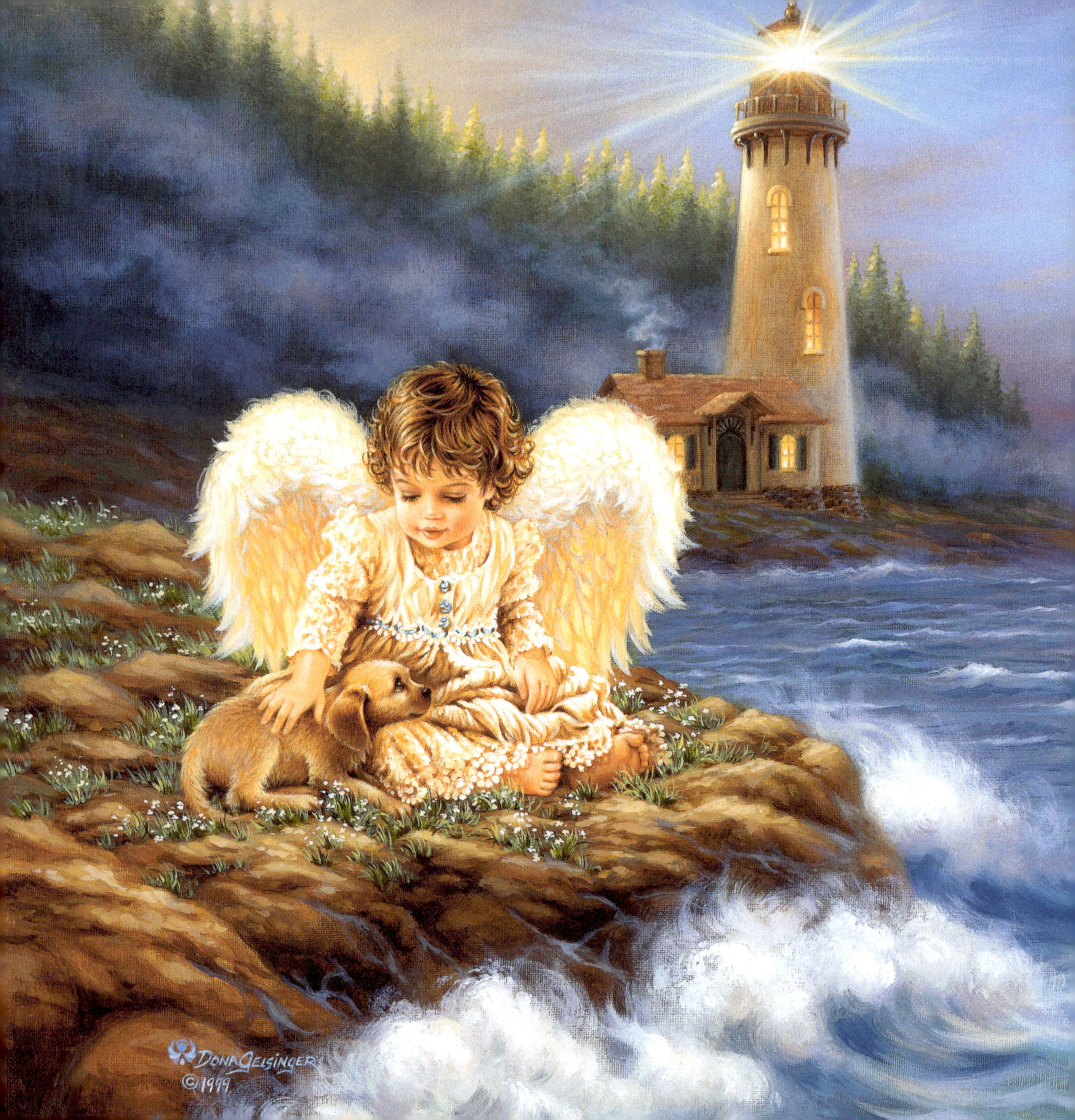
DonaGelsinger
©1999

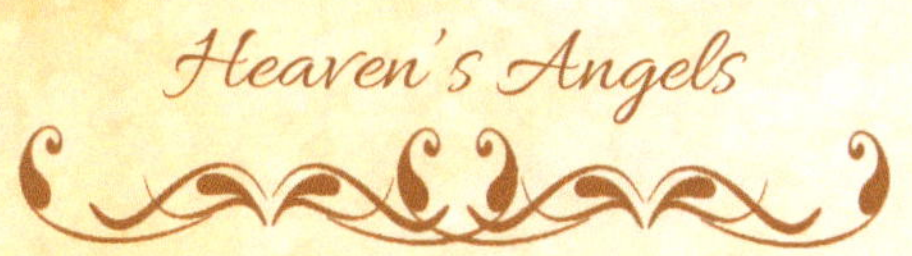

The Virtues

When you feel like you are reaching the depths of despair, call out to God and ask for help. He will send you the choir of **Virtues** to intercede as a bright light to your darkness. This choir of Angels can perform miracles that are greater than you can imagine. Virtues are given the power to carry out the Will of God in order to accomplish the ordering of nature.

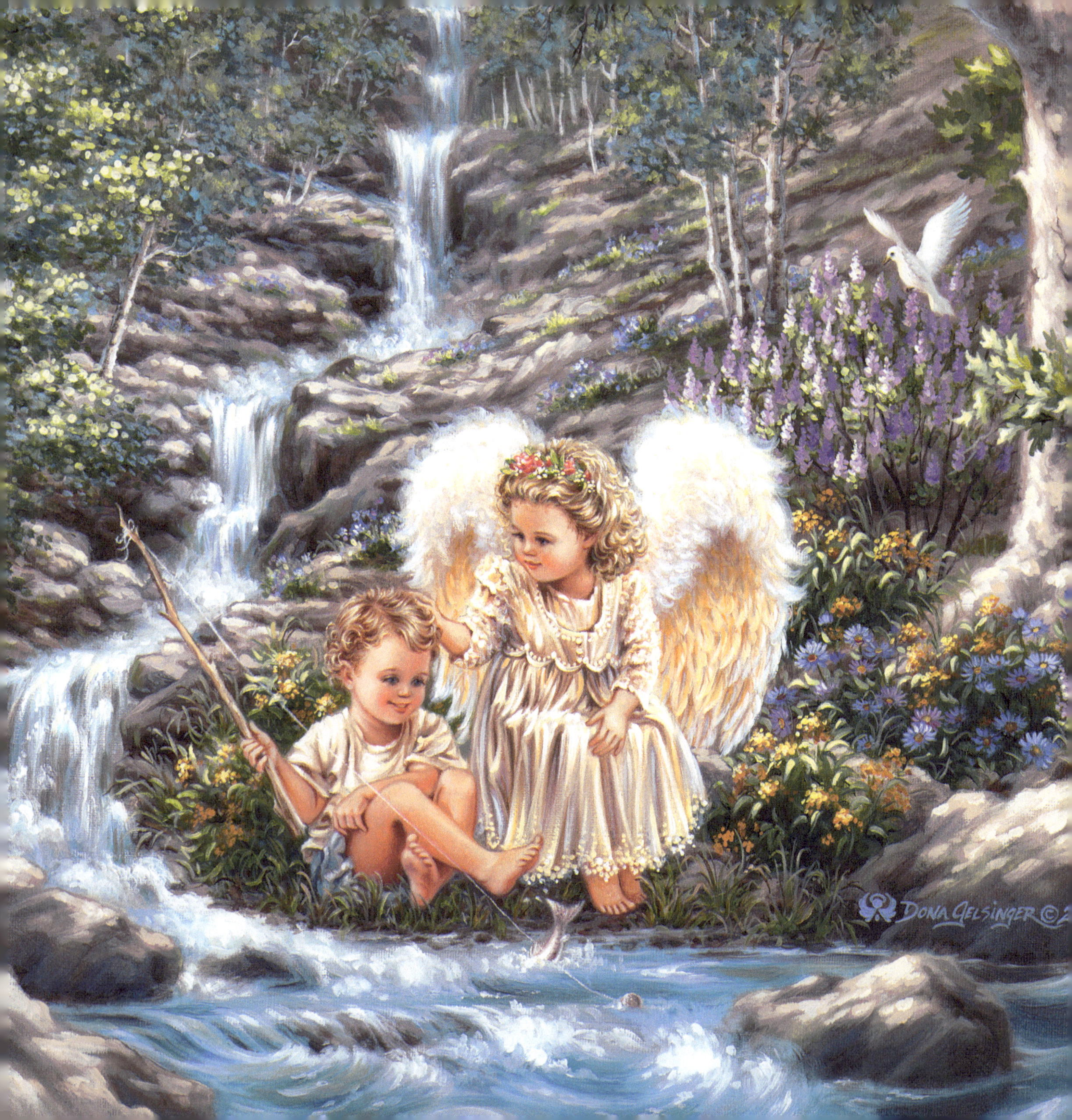

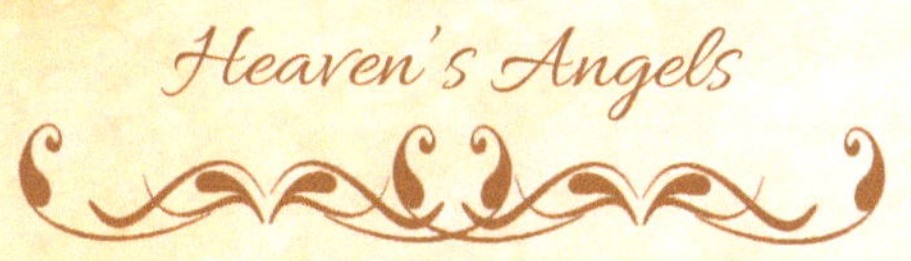

How can the human mind contemplate the mysteries of creation that are from an uncreated God? The human mind can only behold that which is experienced and can only understand familiar things throughout its lifespan. Humans cannot explain how to measure a bushel of wind; that which is unseen cannot be explained, but only felt. When a miracle occurs in your world, do not try to put words to it: it is a gift of the Virtues. Increase your faith and believe in the unbelievable. Then, you will be enlightened to God's ways.

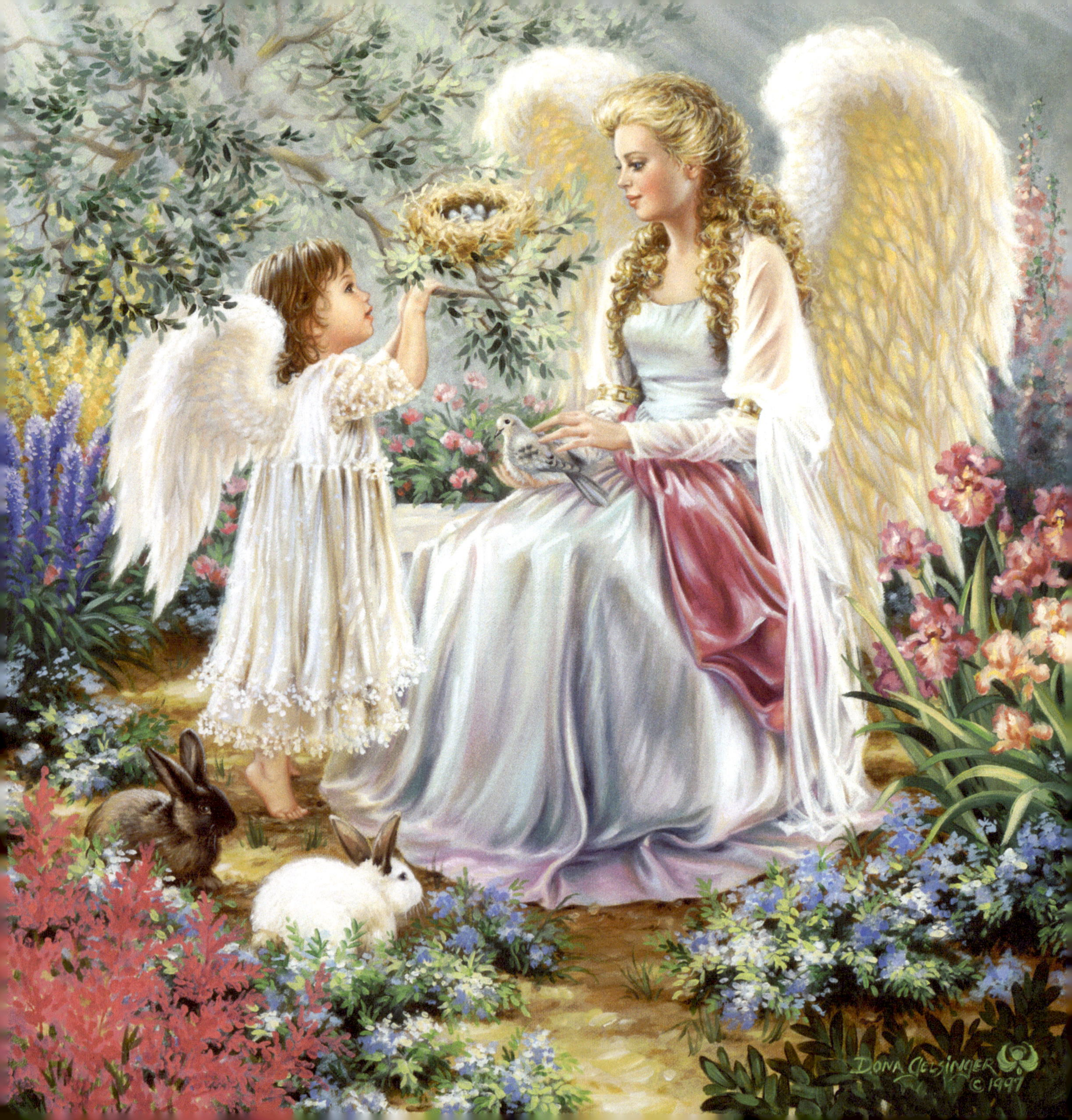

DONA GELSINGER
©1997

The Powers

Once God gives His command to the angelic choirs, the **Powers** act. They have the duty to delegate how to execute what has been commanded and direct the lower choirs in keeping order in creation while protecting it from being overthrown by Satan. The Powers are like the conductor of a symphony who instructs the musicians on which notes they must play in order to harmonize them all into a beautiful masterpiece. As we travel throughout time and space and the eternal now of the heavens, the orchestra of melodious sounds is heard echoing throughout creation. Each of the senses is heightened to the sights and sounds of infinite bliss. Beyond that beauty, though, the spiritual war is carrying on, and the Powers are protecting the earth by fighting against the evil spirits who attempt to destroy creation by tempting the free will of the human soul with sin.

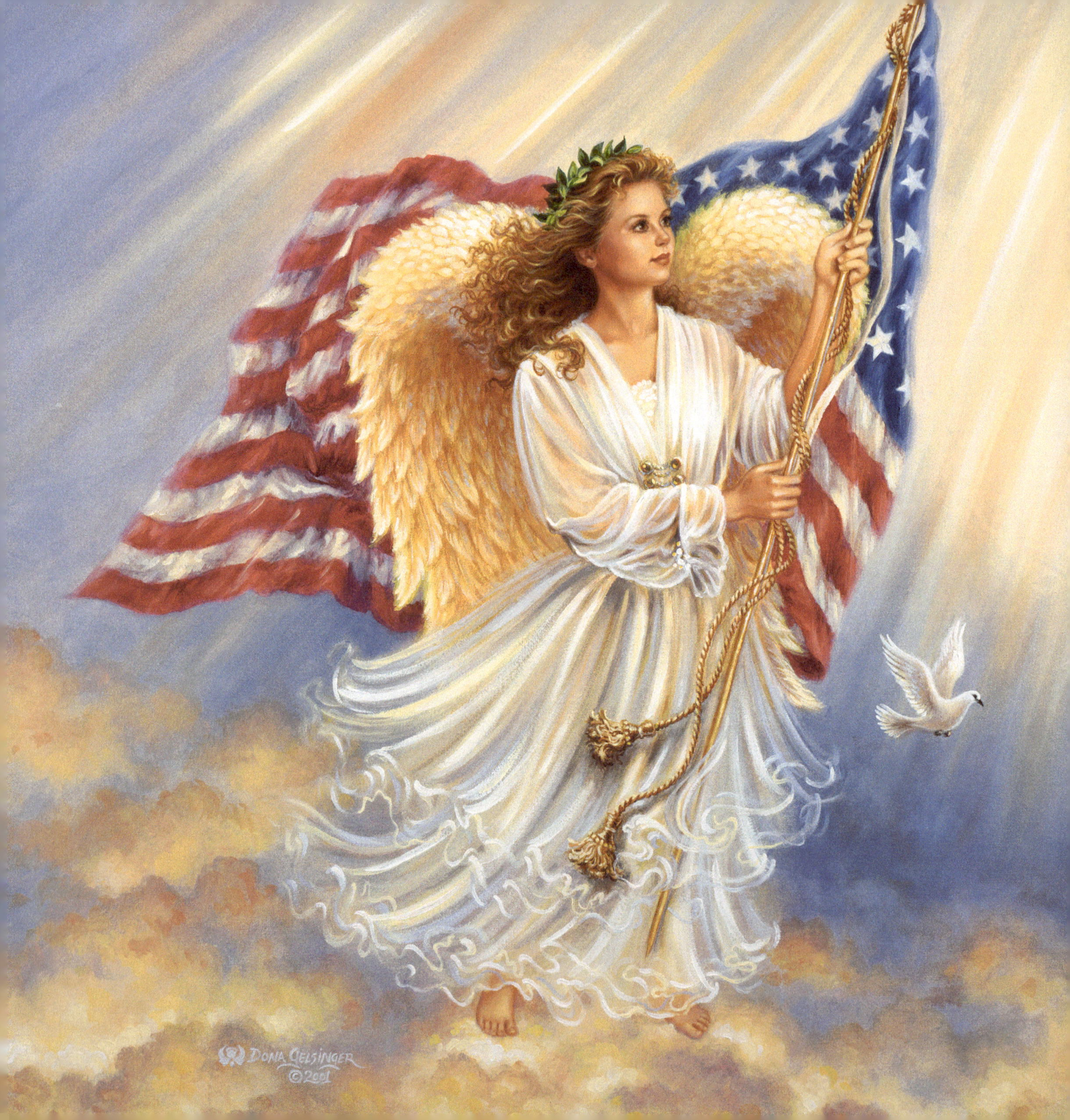

DONA GELSINGER
©2001

THE THIRD HIERARCHY

The Principalities

Every kingdom, nation, community, and leader is protected by the **Principalities**. There was once a man named Ezra who asked many questions regarding the ways of God. He was troubled by the destruction of Jerusalem thirty years before, and the thriving land of Babylon whose sins he saw were insurmountably heavier than the rest of the world. But when God sent me, Uriel, to ask him, "How do you weigh a pound of fire?" he could not answer. Yet, fire was something that he had known since he was a child.

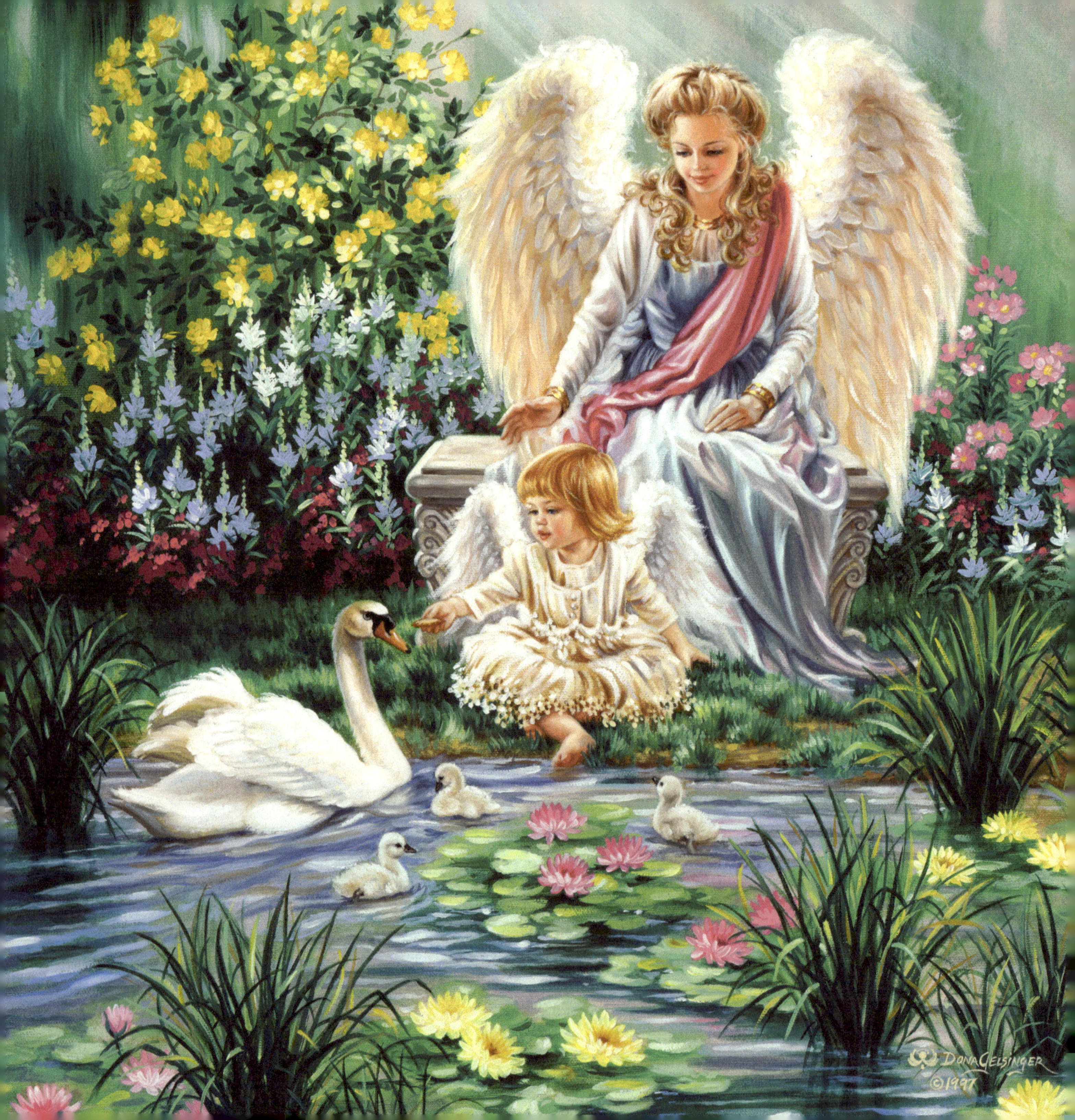

Dona Gelsinger
©1997

You see, your human nature cannot embrace the understanding of heavenly things. Only heavenly beings can understand the ways of God. Therefore, when leaders rise to power by means that seem sinful in nature, trust that the Principalities stand watch over them and can only inspire their minds, but not change the will of their hearts. Principalities will protect religion and give strength during times of hardship. Throughout time, these angels have sought to raise worthy people to honorable offices for the sake of spreading God's glory. In the end, it is written how the battle will be won.

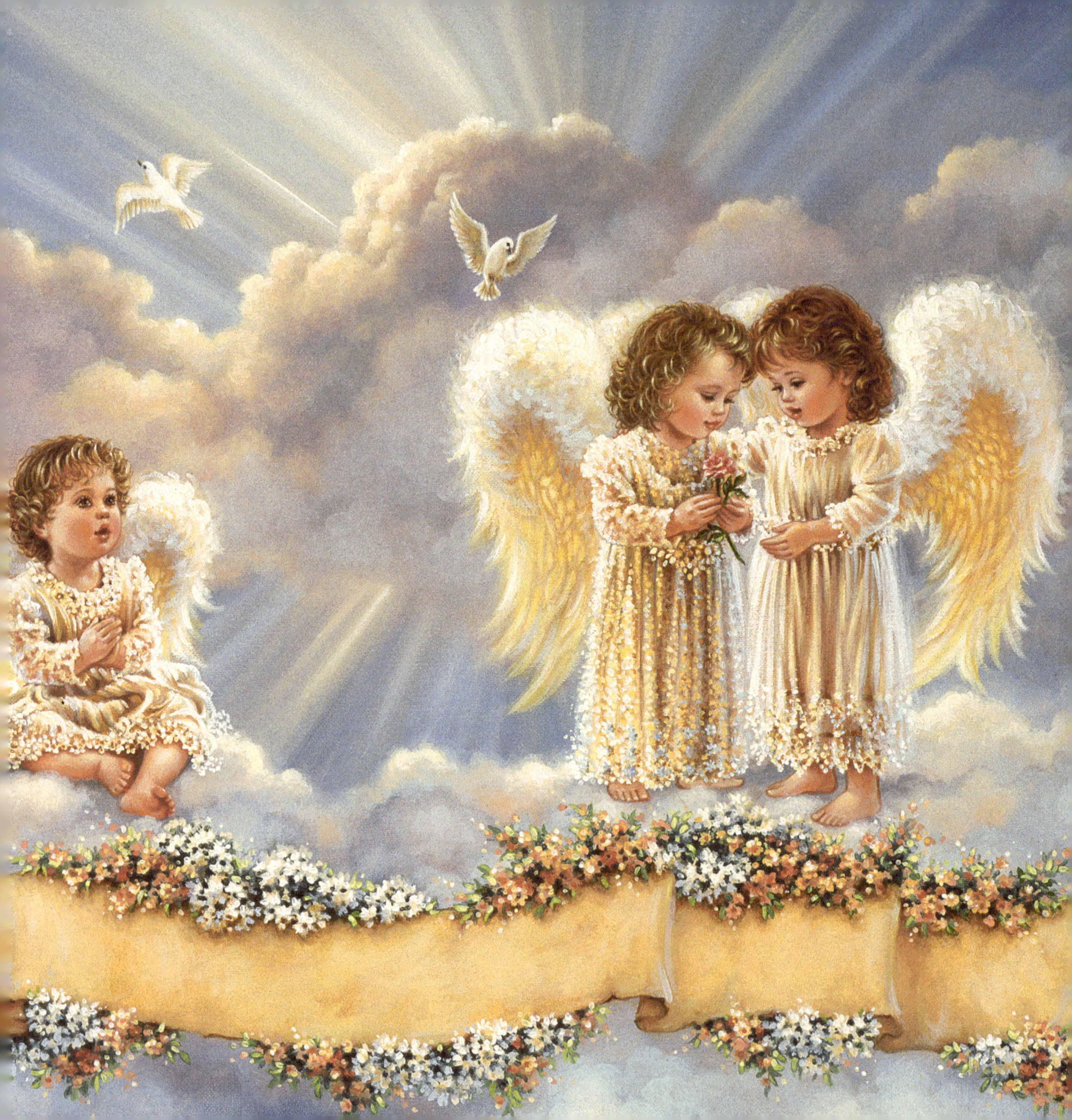

The Archangels

My fellow **Archangels** and I are the leaders of the angelic armies. Michael is our Captain, whose courage and protection never cease. In the end, he will lead the final battle with the keys to the vast abyss; into this he will cast Satan and his followers, never to tempt or torture man again. As I soar alongside our warrior Prince Michael, ushering in justice and truth during the last days, we have as our Archangel Brothers Gabriel and Raphael. When God revealed His plan to His humble servant, Mary, whose womb would hold the Father's incarnate Son, He sent His Ambassador Gabriel with the message of Divine Love. Raphael was sent to Tobit as a great physician who helps heal the mind, body, and spirit.

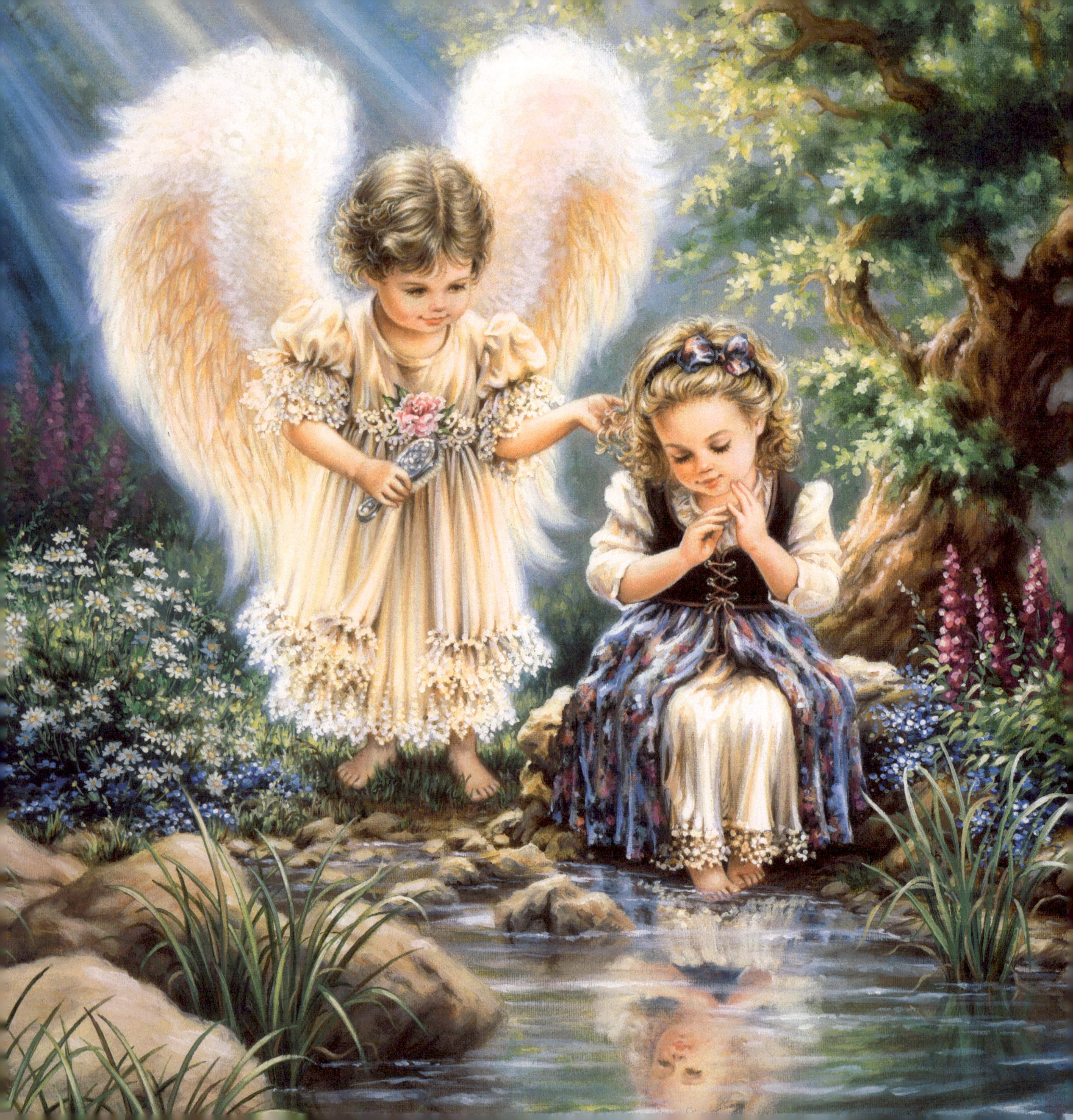

Together we stand to protect the Church against her enemies and keep the movements of men and the world at peace. We reveal prophecies and grant enlightenment with the light of knowledge to anyone who seeks the Truth. Through inspiration, we can help strengthen faith by granting an understanding of God's Will. We can help you unlock the mysteries of God's ways by showing you the laws of creation and the world around you. A whole new world where Heaven and Earth become one awaits the believing mind; you just need to open your heart in faith.

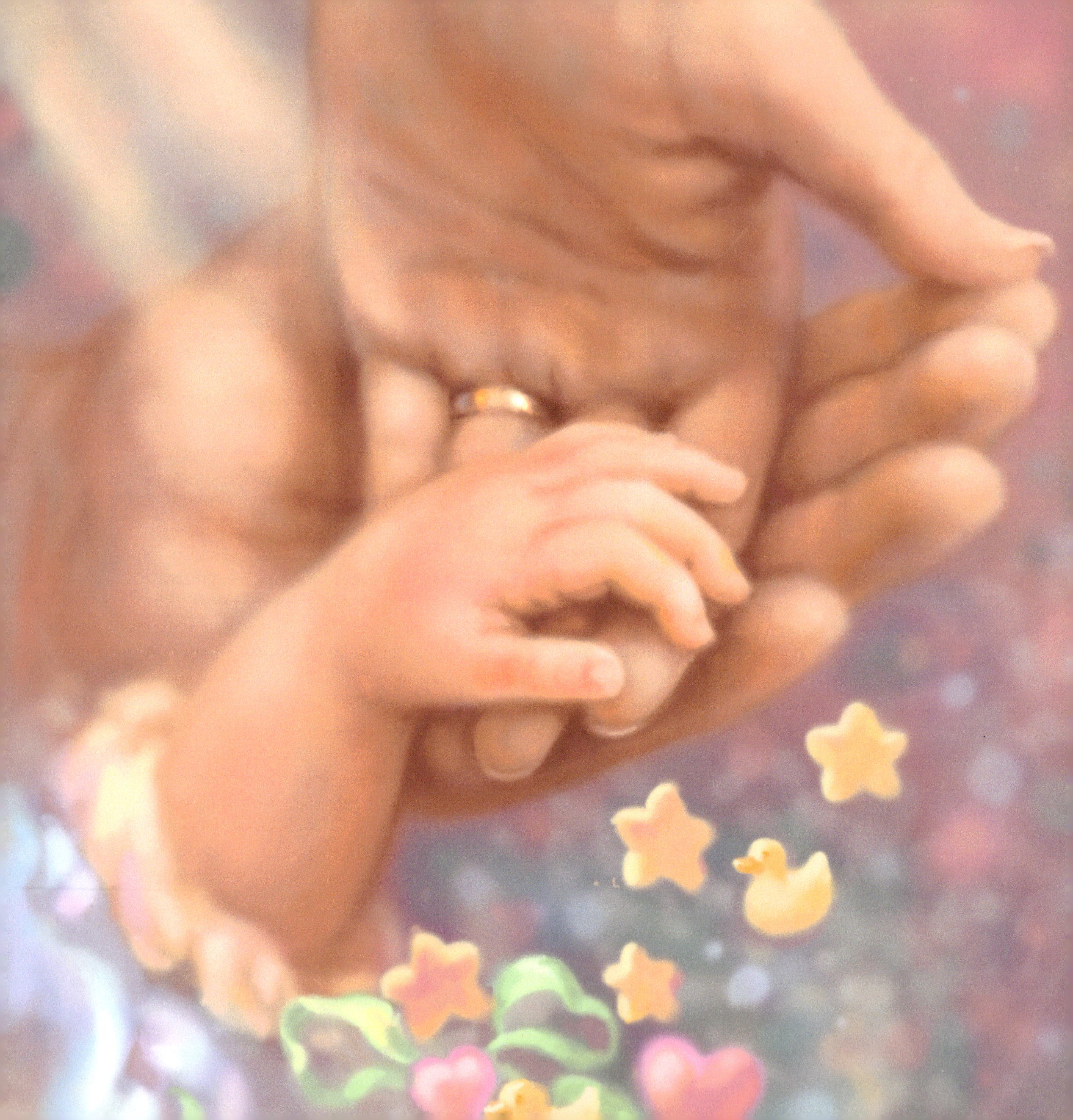

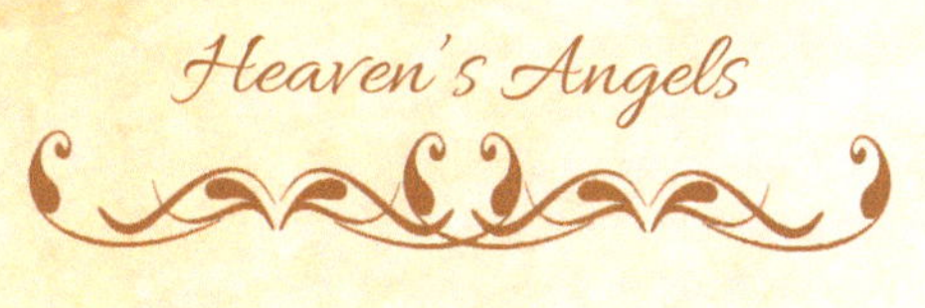

The Angels

The **Angels** have communicated most ardently with man throughout time. They are God's most comprehensive messengers who carry out His plan with mankind. At the moment of conception, every soul is given an Angel to act as guardian and protector.

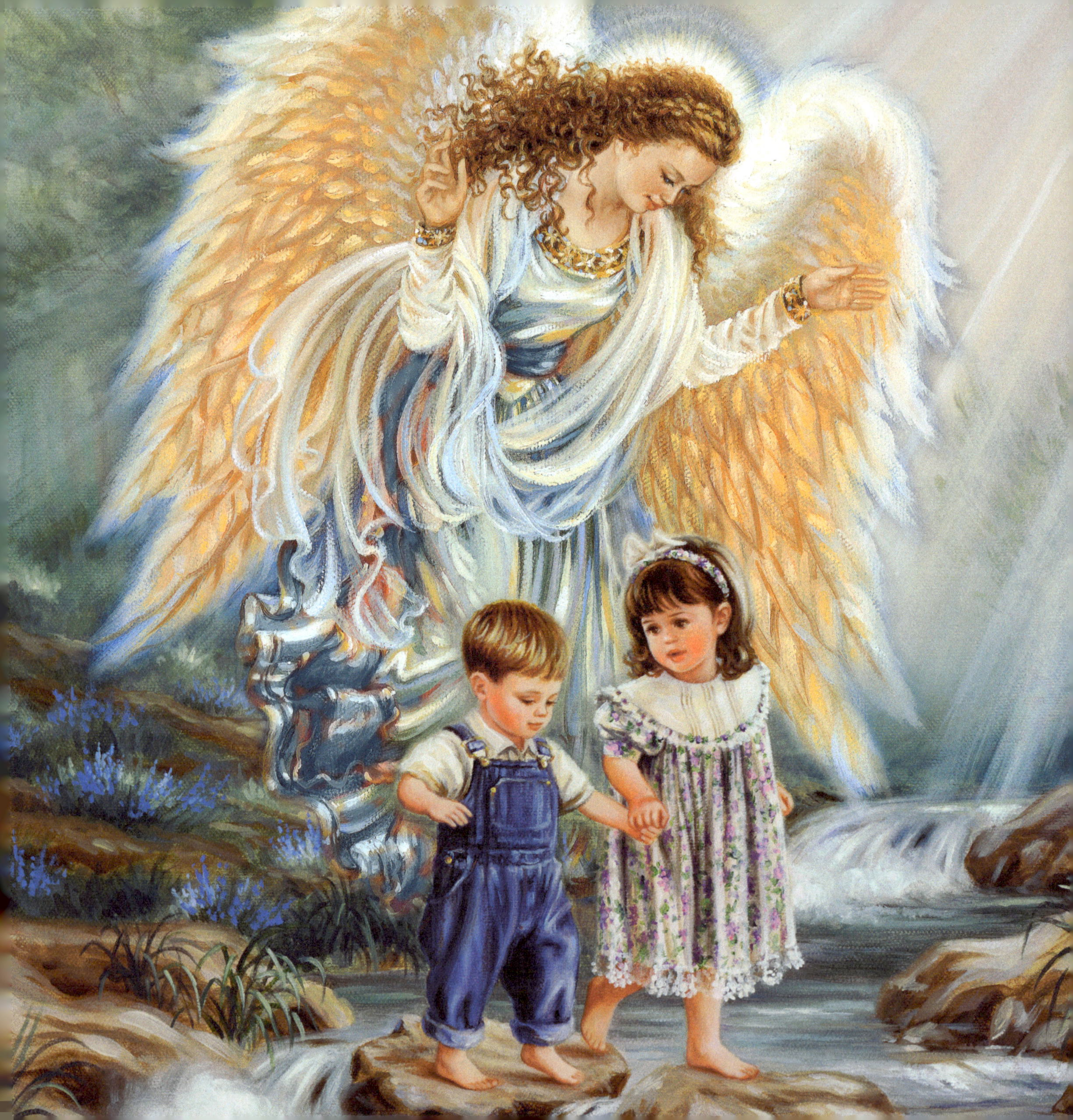

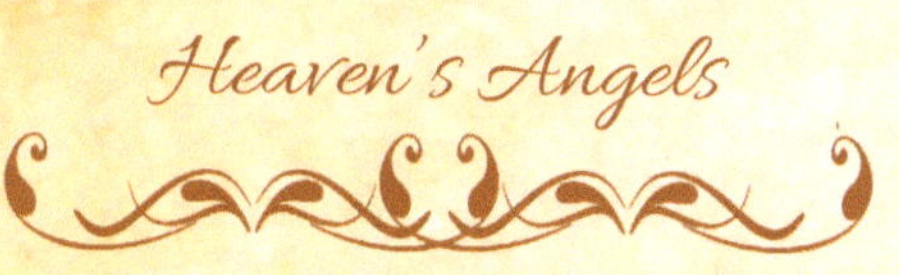

God has also entrusted His Angels with the task of guiding His children to help them overcome any obstacles that they are facing. But most importantly, they teach children virtues, which are the standards for living life with moral excellence. When you practice virtues, you build a foundation that will help you make good choices. The more virtuous you become, the more you love God and your neighbors. Then, one day you will reach Heaven.

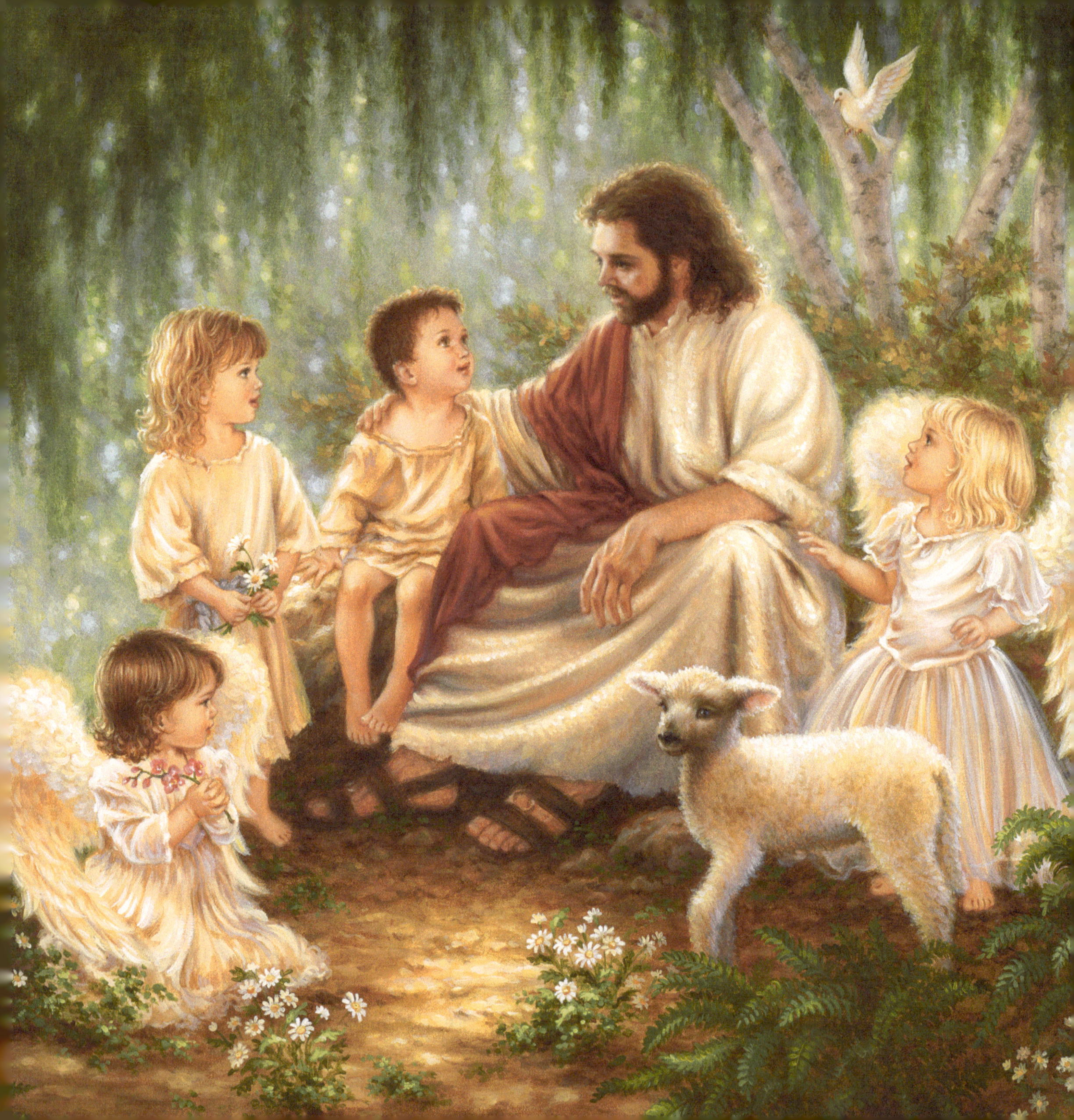

Your Guardian Angel is charged with keeping watch over your soul and never leaving your side. At the Final Judgment, your Angel must bring to the Lord every cell in your body so that your body and soul can be reunited. Your prayers are heard by God because your Guardian Angel brings them to His throne, and He returns with His answer for you. Even if you get an answer that you do not want to hear or do not get an answer at all, that is still God's answer and one day He will reveal His plan for you. Each day the Father gives a gift to your Angel for you to receive; all you have to do is ask. It not only helps you throughout your life, but also in death it will comfort and assist you.

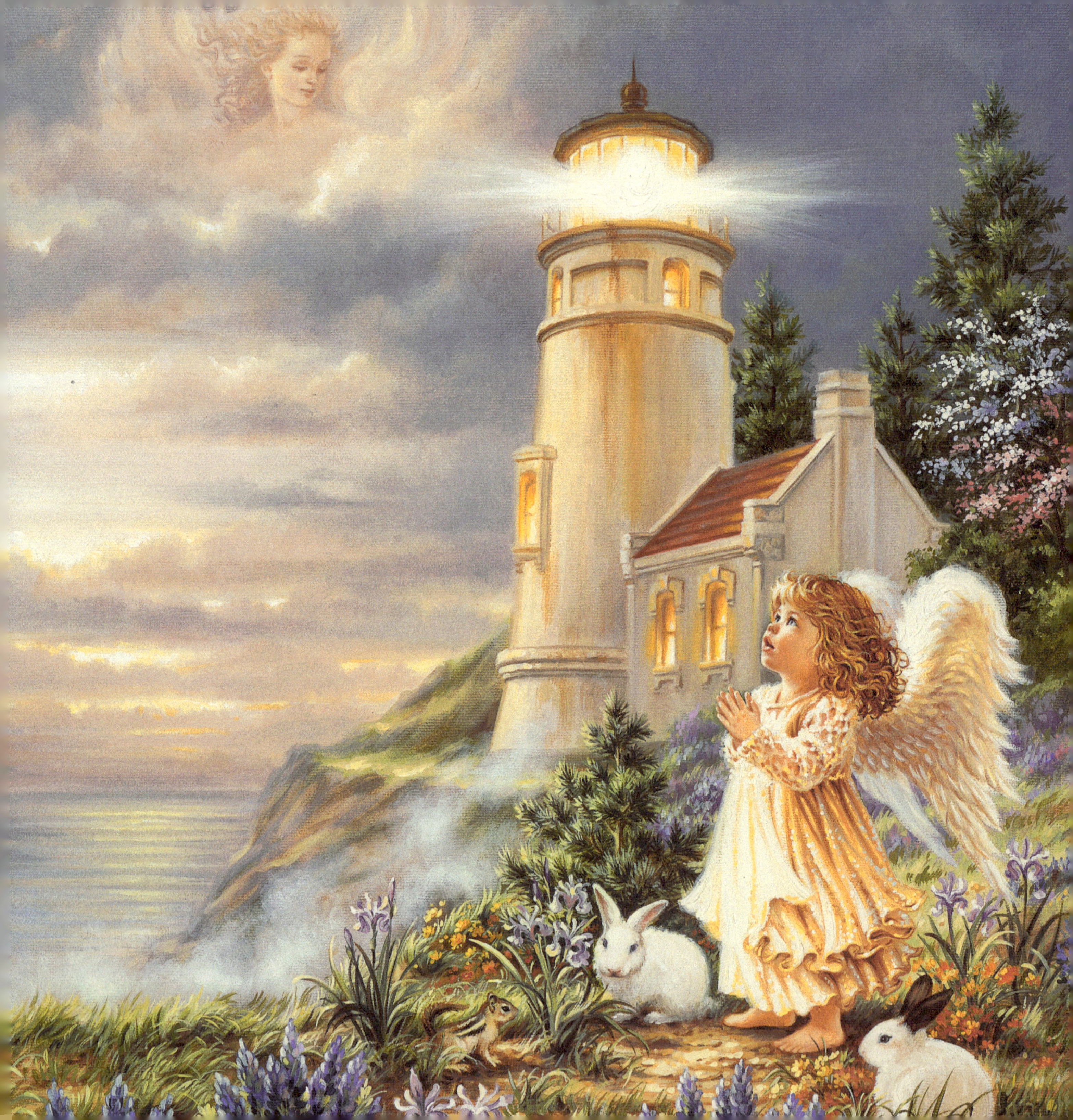

When you get to Heaven, your final destination, you will meet every one of your ancestors back to your first parents, Adam and Eve. You will see how we are all connected like golden rings throughout time that will continue to the last person in your lineage. At times, with God's permission, your ancestors will ask the Angels to reach through time and space to remind you of the importance of your ancestors' existence, and their impact on your life today.

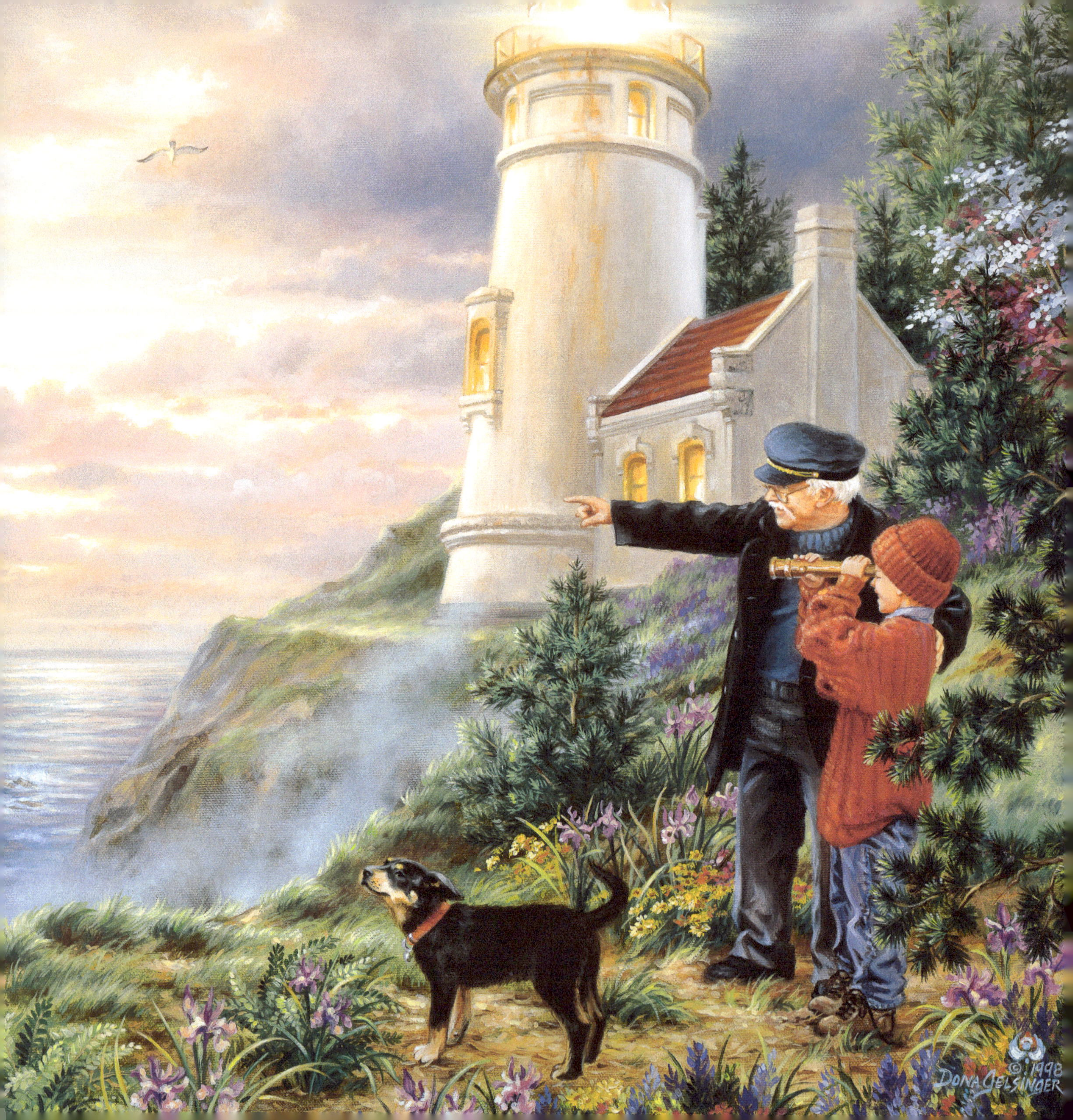

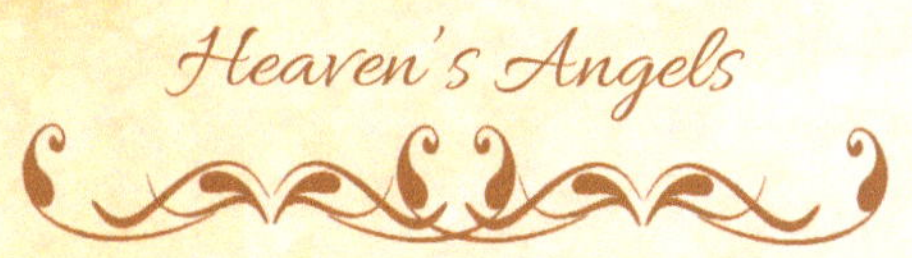

When a thought of your loved one suddenly pops into your mind; you hear a favorite song on the radio; you come across a picture that randomly appears; or you notice something that you didn't see before as a reminder of them — know in your heart that these are not mere coincidences but "Godincidences." They are gifts to affirm that your loved ones are always there beyond the veil. They will intercede in prayer for you at the Throne of the Lord and be there to rejoice with you in your return home.

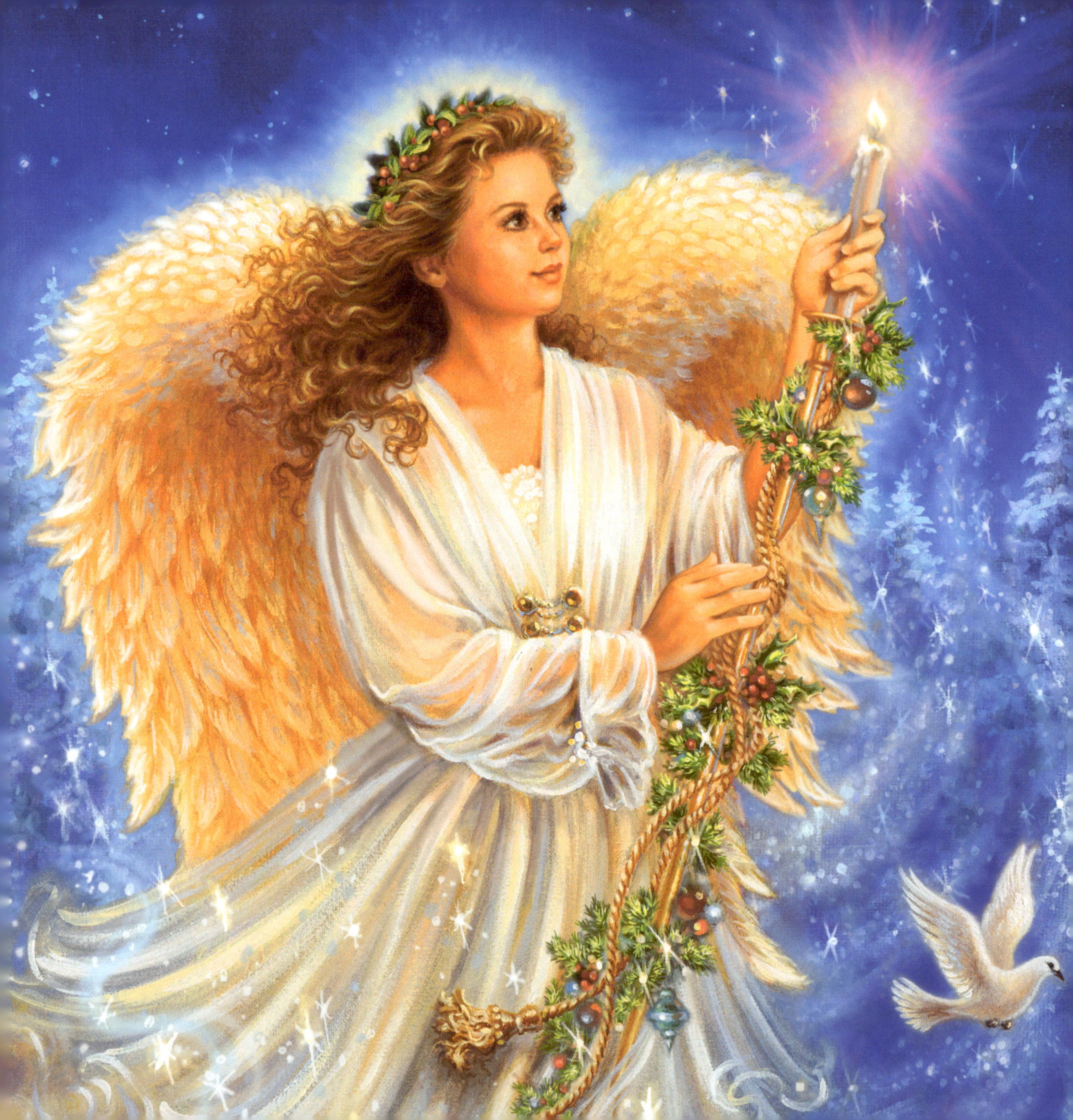

St. Uriel's Promise of Hope

Darkness is a lie to fool the eye. I've been to the depths of blackness and have always found the light of God there waiting. I was witness to horrible events in the world dating back to the beginning. I saw the world created the way it was intended to be, and I witnessed the first fall of man because of his pride. I stood at the gates of the Garden and counseled man to then live with free will, and watched as he chose not to live in accordance with God's Will. I have the sword of truth and will bring it to any given situation to help enlighten your soul and illuminate the darkness, if only you will ask.

INSPIRATIONAL AND CATECHETICAL BASIS

The inspirations for this explanation of the Angels and their hierarchies are based on Holy Scripture and Catholic doctrine that states that within the realm of angels, there is a hierarchy. In addition, the following resources were used:

- The Summa Theologica I:108, written by St. Thomas Aquinas, considered as "The Doctor of the Angels" is a source that unites the theology of the East and the West as it follows St. Denis (De Coelesti Hierarchia, vi, vii) and St. Gregory. It divides the angels into three hierarchies each of which contains three orders. Their proximity to the Supreme Being serves as the basis of this division. In the first hierarchy he places the Seraphim, Cherubim, and Thrones; in the second, the Dominations, Virtues, and Powers; in the third, the Principalities, Archangels, and Angels.

- The only Scriptural names furnished to individual angels are Raphael, Michael, and Gabriel, names which signify their respective attributes. Apocryphal Jewish Books, such as the Book of Enoch, supply those of Uriel and Jeremiel. Many others are found in other apocryphal sources. Archangel Uriel is the fourth Archangel whose name is referred to as "the flaming sword" in Biblical text. He is revered in Eastern Orthodox Christianity and Eastern Catholicism and is found in the Bible in the Second Book of Esdras, Genesis 3: 24, and Matthew 28:2.

- In addition, writings by Dionysius the Areopagite, also considered a Father on the Angels because he walked the earth with the Holy Apostle Paul, are believed to reveal angelic mysteries through Divine revelation.

- The Angels Magazine http://stmichaelthearchangel.us/

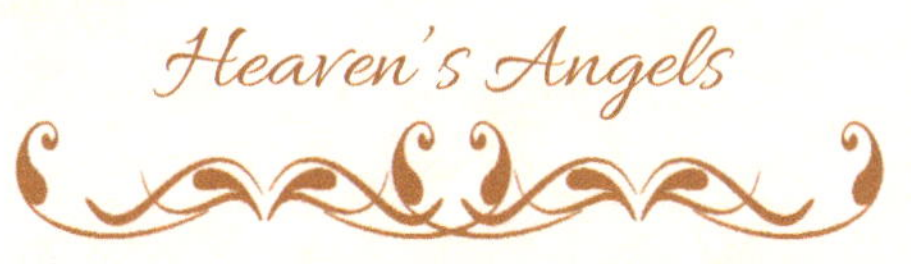

Thank you

To my husband Jason, thank you for your love and faith in this project and your patience through it all. You are my rock! I love you with my whole heart and soul, eternally. Thank you to my children Alina, Carina, Kristina and Andrew for inspiring me to want to teach you about the angels. *I love you forever; I like you for always; as long as I'm living my babies you'll be!* To Brian, David, Steven, Kathryn, Zyla, Landon, Zachary, Valerie and all my family, friends and those of you who have touched my life in any way, thank you for your support, inspiration, and advice throughout the years. Thank you Maxine for being my sister in Christ. To my grandparents who first introduced me to the angels through the beautiful renditions of the Heaven's Angel's series by Dona Gelsinger, I am grateful.

Thank you to Jesse Gelsinger for your never-ending support, friendship and guidance, your expertise is invaluable. Dona Gelsinger, your gift is divinely inspired, and I am grateful that you share your gifts with others. It has been my honor that my words can be visually expressed through your artwork. Thank you Jesus, for your Holy Guidance given through your angelic messengers. Thank you Mom, Dad, Busia, Eddie, Christy, Jacque, Mike, Charlene, Mom (Lynda), Dad (Paul), Jeff and Margie Baker, Mike Barone, Leslie Malek, Blair Crombie, Grace Kukunis, Jessica Bardin, Alexa Castillo and Paula Martin for your love, support, editorial guidance and reviews. Thank you to my St. Gabriel Catholic Radio family for all your love and support throughout the years. Thank you Jennifer Bitler of Doxology Design and Robert Sims of Biblio Publishing for the

layout and design. Your gifts are what this project needed to weave together my words with Dona Gelsinger's artwork. Fr. Thomas Blau, I am so appreciative that you are in my life. Thank you for assuring that my fundamental interpretation of the Summa Theologica was at least somewhat close to what St. Thomas Aquinas was trying to say! To all the children, the unborn babies and those who have suffered from infant loss, I hope this story brings you hope that you are never alone. God be with you; sleep with the angels. St. Thomas Aquinas, St. Michael, St. Uriel, Mary Undoer of Knots, St. Theresa, Nani, Poppop, Grandma Anna and Grandpa John, Jaja and all the holy souls, angels and saints, especially my guardian angel — Pray for us.

(To all my family and friends, I know I have forgotten to name some of you — please forgive me and know you are in my heart of thanks.)